Saving the American Wilderness

Look for these and other books in the Lucent Overview Series:

Saving the American Wilderness

by Ann Malaspina

OUR ENDANGERED PLANET

LUCENT *Overview Series*

LUCENT *Overview Series*

Library of Congress Cataloging-in-Publication Data

Malaspina, Ann
    Saving the American Wilderness / by Ann Malaspina.
       p.   cm. — (Lucent overview series)
    Includes bibliographical references and index.
    Summary: Discusses saving the American wilderness, including preservation and conservation, environmental activism, recreation in the wilderness, and the future of wilderness management.
    ISBN 1-56006-505-2   (lib. bdg. : alk. paper)
    1. Wilderness areas—Environmental aspects—United States—Juvenile literature.   2. Wilderness areas—United States—Recreational use—Juvenile literature.   3. Wilderness areas—United States—Management—Juvenile literature. [1. Wilderness areas. 2. Conservation of natural resources.] I. Title. II. Series.
GV191.4.M25   1999
333.78'2'0973—dc21
                                            98-31959
                                              CIP
                                              AC

Contents

Introduction

THE EVERGLADES NATIONAL Park in South
Florida is one of the most fragile wildlands in the United
States. Comprising freshwater and saltwater flows, open
saw-grass prairies, coral reefs, and islands of pine, cypress,
and mangrove forests, this 1.5-million-acre subtropical
wilderness is home to ibis, roseate spoonbills, wood storks,
manatees, the saltwater crocodile, and myriad other
wildlife. The Everglades, along with the larger Everglades
ecosystem, is also in serious trouble.

The century-old crusade to drain South Florida's
swamps and convert water and grass into farmland and real
estate has nearly destroyed this unique ecosystem, thought
to be the largest freshwater marsh in the world. "The Everglades were treated as a commodity . . . and developers reduced a natural work of art to a thing pedestrian and
mundane," said Senator Bob Graham, the former Florida
governor who began the Save the Everglades Campaign in
1983.[1] Once encompassing more than 10,700 square miles,
the Everglades, which is really a slow-moving stream of
shallow water and saw grass flowing from its headwaters
near present-day Orlando south to the Gulf of Mexico, Bis-
cayne Bay, and Florida Bay, has shrunk to less than half its
original size.

Damaged by urban development, toxic runoff from sugarcane and dairy farming, and government drainage and
flood control dams and levees, the Everglades' future is in
jeopardy. Populations of wood storks, egrets, and other
long-legged wading birds that nest in the Everglades have

The Florida Everglades has been a focal point in the battle to protect America's remaining undeveloped areas.

fallen by 93 percent since the 1920s. Fourteen animal species in the Everglades, including the Florida panther, wood stork, snail kite, and American crocodile, are threatened or endangered. The water, which is the sole drinking-water source for over 5 million people in South Florida, has dangerously high levels of mercury, phosphorous, and nitrogen.

The fight for the Everglades

As in many other environmental crises, the call for action to save the Everglades came from ordinary citizens. In 1905, Guy Bradley, hired by the National Audubon Society, was killed while protecting heron and egret rookeries from plume hunters, fueling a public campaign to protect the wading bird colonies. Ernest F. Coe, a Yale-educated landscape architect who loved the Everglades, wrote to the National Park Service in 1928 proposing a national park for the area. Congress passed a park bill in 1934, but the Great Depression and World War II stalled the plan.

In 1947, a former newspaper reporter named Marjory Stoneman Douglas published her classic book, *The Everglades: River of Grass*, which stirred the public to recognize

The American crocodile is one of the many species that is threatened by development around the Everglades.

just what was being lost. That same year, President Harry Truman dedicated the Everglades National Park, though it was a fraction of the size put forward by park advocates. The Everglades was the first park set aside solely for its wilderness and wildlife. But months before the park's creation, the Army Corps of Engineers had begun a flood-control project that would drain the swamps and inflict serious ecological damage.

When a jetport was planned for the Big Cypress Swamp in the center of the Everglades in 1969, Douglas founded Friends of the Everglades, a citizens group that became a powerful voice for protecting the ecosystem. The jetport was not built. Yet despite successful efforts by Friends of the Everglades and other environmental groups to clean up Lake Okeechobee and restore the Kissimmee River, which feed the Everglades, in the late 1990s, the vast ecosystem is still under siege. The Florida Bay, which relies on clean water from the Everglades marshes, is hypersalty and choked with algae.

In 1988, the U.S. Attorney's Office sued Florida for failing to protect the water entering the national park from agricultural pollution. Three years later, Florida settled the lawsuit, but sugarcane farmers contested the agreement, and lengthy negotiations ensued. Finally, on May 3, 1994, Florida's Everglades Forever Act was signed, ending thirty-six lawsuits and providing funds to save the Everglades. In 1997, the Clinton administration and state of Florida agreed to pay $133.5 million for fifty thousand acres of sugarcane land to create a buffer of reservoirs and marshes to protect the Everglades from agricultural pollution.

Restoration

The Army Corps of Engineers and the South Florida Water Management District are now developing a comprehensive multibillion-dollar restoration plan, which includes a huge replumbing project to bring back the flow of fresh, clear water to the Everglades. In October 1998, Vice President Al Gore announced plans for an $8 billion network of reservoirs and channels to restore some of the flow of the Everglades and recapture the fresh water that is being lost at sea. The proposed network of channels and reservoirs would provide water for South Florida's growing population and protect the Everglades from further destruction. Meanwhile, park advocates are embroiled in a new battle over plans to turn an air force reserve base in Dade County into a commercial airport, which could bring 250,000 planes a year roaring over the Everglades.

Without the determination of conservationists to save this vulnerable wilderness, much more would surely have been destroyed. Nearly 1 million people visit the Everglades National Park each year, and they do see some signs of hope. The roseate spoonbill, a long-legged wading bird, has recovered from twenty-five nesting pairs in 1947 to as many as one thousand pairs today. As Marjory Stoneman Douglas, who died at the age of 108 in 1998, wrote over fifty years ago: "Perhaps even in this last hour, in a new relation of usefulness and beauty, the vast, magnificent, subtle and unique region of the Everglades may not be utterly lost."[2]

1

Preservation vs. Conservation

WHEN JOHN MUIR, the explorer and naturalist, hiked through the Hetch Hetchy Valley, he was captivated by the untouched wilderness that surrounded him. The remote valley lay some twenty miles north of Yosemite Valley in California's Sierra Nevada. The Tuolumne Indians who lived and hunted in the area called the fertile valley Hetch Hetchy, which means "a grass with edible seeds." By 1868, when Muir first trekked through the Sierra and made his home as a shepherd in the high country, only an occasional hiker or hunter who wandered along the isolated canyon knew of the stunning waterfalls and lush plant growth that made it so remarkable.

Muir saw the Tuolumne River as it tumbled over rocks through a deep gorge, lined with high rock walls colored yellow and red with lichens and shaded by live oaks and pine trees. "For miles the river is one wild, exulting, onrushing mass of snowy purple bloom," wrote Muir in 1890.[3] Surrounding the river were meadows blooming in season with lilies, larkspurs, rock ferns, and plenty of food for grizzly bears and other wildlife. "The whole valley was a charming garden when I last saw it," wrote Muir.[4]

Muir convinced Congress to include the pristine wilderness within the boundaries of the new Yosemite National Park in 1890. But in a few more years, San Francisco's search for a new source of water would ignite a fierce debate over a plan to dam the river to create a municipal dam and reservoir. This dispute forged a lasting schism in the fledgling campaign to save the American wilderness.

On one side of the controversy were preservationists, like Muir, who believed that the Hetch Hetchy Valley and other wild areas should remain forever undisturbed. Proponents of the dam, however, included conservationists like President Theodore Roosevelt, who wanted to save and manage the nation's natural resources, whether water or lumber or minerals, for use by people. Both groups recognized the intrinsic value of the wilderness, but they could not agree on what should become of it.

The preservationists

Muir was not alone in his concern about the vanishing wilderness. By the mid–nineteenth century, the American wilderness, which seemed limitless to the early European settlers and westward pioneers, was under siege. The extinction of many animal species signaled the

John Muir was one of America's first preservationists. He was instrumental in the creation of the first national parks.

vulnerability of nature in a rapidly developing nation. An estimated 15 million bison roamed the western plains in 1865, but in a mere twenty years, a booming market in buffalo hides and the expansion of the western railroad, providing easy transportation of the hides to urban markets, threatened to decimate the herds. Likewise, the pioneers discovered that passenger pigeons, once so plentiful that the flocks darkened the sky during migratory season, were good sources of meat, fat, and feathers. By the 1880s, professional pigeon hunters had nearly wiped out the species, and the last passenger pigeon died in the Cincinnati Zoological Garden in 1914.

The nation's forests were also disappearing. The Europeans who arrived on the East Coast in the early 1600s

The Hetch Hetchy Valley was one of the first places to be designated as a national park.

could have walked through an immense forest stretching thousands of miles from the Atlantic Ocean to the grasslands of the Great Plains. In the next 150 years, most of New England's forest had been cleared for agriculture; the timber used for building and fuel. By 1800, the forests were almost gone. "Farmers and woodcutters had stripped entire watersheds in southern New Hampshire and southern Maine. Woodcutters had to search ever farther inland for the precious pine," write David Dobbs and Richard Ober in *The Northern Forest*.[5]

The early settlers feared wild nature and saw it as an enemy to be conquered and driven back. *Mayflower* passenger William Bradford called the new land a "hideous and desolate wilderness" that needed to be tamed.[6] To survive, the settlers had to cut down trees and protect themselves from wild animals. Wilderness historian Roderick Nash writes in *Wilderness and the American Mind*, "Safety and comfort, even necessities like food and shelter, depended on overcoming the wild environment."[7]

But by the early nineteenth century, some writers and intellectuals began to celebrate the wilderness as a source of innocence, inspiration, and spiritual energy. In his famous 1836 essay, "Nature," writer and philosopher Ralph Waldo Emerson wrote, "In the woods, too, a man casts off his years, as the snake his slough, and at what period soever of life, is always a child."[8] People should live in harmony with nature, and gather inspiration and wisdom from the flowers, animals, fields, and mountains, Emerson believed.

Walden

Others warned that the clean air and water, abundant forests, and open prairies could no longer be taken for granted. "This winter they are cutting down our woods more seriously than ever. . . . It is a thorough process, this war with the wilderness," wrote Henry David Thoreau, the Massachusetts writer and philosopher, in 1852.[9] Thoreau lived from 1845 to 1847 in a hut he built at Walden Pond near his home in Concord. In his book *Walden* (1854), he described the changing seasons and his respect for the natural world:

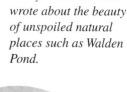

Henry David Thoreau wrote about the beauty of unspoiled natural places such as Walden Pond.

> There are few traces of man's hands to be seen. The water laves the shore as it did a thousand years ago. A lake is the landscape's most beautiful and expressive feature. It is earth's eye.[10]

Thoreau lamented what he saw as people's destruction of nature, particularly the felling of trees in the forests of Maine and Massachusetts, and the loss of wildlands. "The West of which I speak is but another name for the Wild, and what I have been proposing to say is, that in Wildness is the preservation of the World," he wrote in "Walking," an essay published in the *Atlantic Monthly* in 1862.[11]

Muir, who admired Thoreau, also realized that wild nature was essential, not

just for its beauty but for its role in communities of living things and their physical habitats—the air, water, and soil that they need to function. Though the term *ecosystem* had not yet been coined, Muir recognized that trees and plants in wilderness areas protect and regulate watersheds, the large areas of land from which rainwater drains into brooks, streams, and major river systems:

> It has been shown over and over again that if these mountains were to be stripped of their trees and underbrush . . . both lowlands and mountains would speedily become little better than deserts. . . . Drought and barrenness would follow.[12]

Wilderness also serves as important habitat for wildlife and protects the biodiversity of animal and plant species. Wildlands help control climate and recycle gases as the plants and trees take carbon dioxide from the air and turn it into oxygen.

Muir spent many years hiking and observing the American wilderness, from the Alaskan glaciers to the Arizona

The clear-cutting of forests, long a practice of timber companies, has a devastating effect on watershed areas and wildlife habitat.

desert. By the 1880s, Muir saw that industrialization, agriculture, and the growth of cities were destroying the wilderness.

Muir urged the government to protect the forests from plundering by timber thieves and uncontrolled logging. In his essay "The American Forests," published in the *Atlantic Monthly*, Muir wrote:

> Any fool can destroy trees. They cannot run away; and if they could, they would still be destroyed—chased and hunted down as long as fun or a dollar could be got out of their bark hides, branching horns, or magnificent bole backbones. . . . Through all the wonderful, eventful centuries since Christ's time—and long before that—God has cared for these trees, saved them from drought, disease, avalanches, . . . but he cannot save them from fools,—only Uncle Sam can do that.[13]

The conservationists

Like Muir and Thoreau, the conservationists also wanted to protect the wilderness. But they wanted to manage or conserve forests, rivers, and mountains so that future generations could continue to profit from lumber, water, minerals, and other resources. Tourism and hunting, too, were viewed by early conservationists as acceptable uses of wilderness because they brought economic benefits.

Many of the early conservationists were wealthy eastern businessmen and industrialists who liked to fish, hunt, and hike, as writer John F. Reiger explains in *American Sportsmen and the Origins of Conservation*. Sportsman and naturalist George Bird Grinnell, founder of the original Audubon Society in 1886 and publisher of *Field and Stream* magazine, was among the first to urge protection for animal habitats. Grinnell and others recognized that game animals needed wilderness areas for survival. A good friend of Grinnell's was Theodore Roosevelt, an amateur naturalist and outdoorsman who liked to hunt bear and buffalo in the West. Roosevelt lived for a time on a ranch in the Little Missouri River valley in South Dakota, where he hunted wapiti and pronghorn antelope on the plains. In the late 1880s, Grinnell and Roosevelt started the Boone and Crockett Club, one of the first organizations to focus on conservation and wildlife preservation. As governor of New York from 1898 to 1900, Roosevelt worked to protect the Adirondacks from overlogging and supported laws to save songbirds from slaughter for hatmakers.

Soon after Roosevelt became president in 1901, following the assassination of President William McKinley, he made conservation an important part of his agenda. In his first annual message to the American people, Roosevelt outlined his goals of forest conservation and preservation, including the use of forest reserves as wildlife preserves. He once declared that conservation of natural resources is "the fundamental problem which underlies almost every other problem of our national life." [14]

Roosevelt urged Americans to use the nation's natural resources wisely, not just for private gain. "I believe that the natural resources must be used for the benefit of all our people and not monopolized for the benefit of the few," he said. [15] However, Roosevelt had no desire to put loggers and ranchers out of business, writes H. W. Brands in his 1997 biography, *T. R.: The Last Romantic;* Roosevelt "advocated allowing forests to be cut for lumber, rangeland to be open to grazing, rivers to be dammed for irrigation and electrical power." [16]

Pelican Island

Yet Roosevelt was also a friend to the wilderness. During his presidency, Roosevelt took many steps to save wildlands. In 1903, he established the first national wildlife refuge, Pelican Island, on the Indian River in Florida, to save imperiled wading birds, and he later created over fifty more refuges, setting the stage for the National Wildlife Refuge System. The refuge system, managed by the U.S. Fish and Wildlife Service, has now grown to 509 refuges with more than 92 million acres of land and water dedicated to wildlife conservation. The popular and gregarious Republican also created the U.S. Forest Service in 1905. In 1907, after Congress, lobbied by the lumber barons, took away the president's power to preserve forests, Roosevelt quickly issued a decree expanding the forest reserve system by 16 million acres before the new law was enacted. "We are prone to speak of the resources of this country as inexhaustible; this is not so," said Roosevelt in 1907.[17]

Despite their differences, the conservationists and preservationists agreed they must act to protect the wilderness. Muir took Roosevelt on a three-day hike through Yosemite in May 1903, and they resolved that the federal government had to move fast to establish more parks and wildlife refuges. Yet Muir found no friend in the Roosevelt White House when controversy erupted over the plan to dam the Tuolumne River.

Hetch Hetchy

By the 1890s, San Francisco, located on a dry coastal peninsula, was chronically short of fresh water. With its population growing fast, the city began looking for sites to develop new reservoirs. About 150 miles from San Francisco, the Tuolumne River flowed through the narrow gorge in the Hetch Hetchy Valley. City engineers studied the possibility of damming the narrow southern end of the valley to create a reservoir.

Outraged that a dam project would be proposed for a national park, Muir led the fight against the reservoir. "These temple destroyers, devotees of ravaging commercialism, seem to have a perfect contempt for Nature, and instead of lifting their eyes to the God of the Mountains, lift them to the Almighty Dollar," wrote an angry Muir in 1912, referring to supporters of the dam.[18]

But Muir could not stop the dam alone. In May 1892, Muir and his supporters founded the Sierra Club, one of the earliest grassroots advocacy groups for the wilderness, to, in his words, "do something for wildness and make the mountains glad."[19] Sierra Club members enjoyed hikes and nature outings, but they also were an influential voice for protecting natural areas.

The Sierra Club delayed but could not defeat the dam. In 1901, under pressure from San Francisco mayor James D. Phelan, Congress passed a right-of-way bill, which for the first time authorized water conduits such as canals, aqueducts, pipelines, and river dams in national parks. The Sierra Club learned of the bill only after its passage. The new law allowed the city to apply to the Interior Department, which oversaw Yosemite National Park, for the rights to the valley.

Gifford Pinchot

Ethan Hitchcock, Roosevelt's secretary of the interior, rejected the Hetch Hetchy project in 1903 and again in 1905. He was determined to keep dams and other utilitarian projects out of the national parks. But in 1905, Gifford Pinchot, President Roosevelt's chief adviser on conservation, became involved in the issue.

Pinchot, a Yale University graduate, was trained in forestry at the French Forest School in Nancy, France, and studied forests in Switzerland and Germany. Forests in these countries in the late nineteenth century were managed by professional foresters as renewable resources. In 1898, Pinchot was appointed chief forester in the U.S. Department of Agriculture, where he set about trying to scientifically manage the nation's forests to survive as profitable sources of timber. "The job was not to stop the axe, but to regulate its use," wrote Pinchot in his 1947 memoir *Breaking New Ground*. But Pinchot also criticized the spoiling of the West by timber companies. "At a time when, in the West, the penalty for stealing a horse was death . . . stealing the public land in open defiance of the law was generally regarded with tolerance or even approval," he wrote.[20] He believed in managing public land for lumber, mining, grazing, and other purposes. Roosevelt named him the first director of the Forest Service in 1905.

An advocate of what he termed the "wise use" of natural resources, Pinchot

Gifford Pinchot, the first director of the U.S. Forest Service.

was convinced that San Francisco's demand for water took precedence over saving a piece of remote wilderness:

> As to my attitude regarding the proposed use of Hetch Hetchy by the city of San Francisco . . . I am fully persuaded that . . . the injury . . . by substituting a lake for the present swampy floor of the valley . . . is altogether unimportant compared with the benefits to be derived from its use as a reservoir.[21]

Faced with growing opposition from Pinchot, Muir appealed to Roosevelt, his onetime hiking companion and friend. Roosevelt asked the Interior Department to look for alternative water sources for San Francisco, but he finally agreed that public opinion favored the dam. "So far everyone that has appeared has been for it and I have been in the disagreeable position of seeming to interfere with the development of the State for the sake of keeping a valley, which apparently hardly anyone wanted to have kept, under national control," Roosevelt wrote in a letter to Muir.[22]

The earthquake that struck San Francisco in 1906 and the fires that followed underscored the city's need for water from Hetch Hetchy.

Hoping to rally support, Muir sent letters to mountaineering clubs and public officials, and published essays in popular magazines. But after the 1906 earthquake, San Francisco burned for three days because broken water lines left the city unable to fight the fires. The city grew even more desperate for water.

Secretary of the Interior James Garfield gave San Francisco the permit to dam Hetch Hetchy in May 1908, but Congress refused to approve the project. Muir had still not given up the fight. After a new president, William Howard Taft, and his secretary of the interior Richard A. Ballinger took office in 1909, Muir invited them on a trip through Yosemite Park and the Hetch Hetchy Valley. Taft hiked from Glacier Point to the valley floor, while Muir lectured him on the importance of saving the valley.

With strong support from San Francisco voters, but not from Muir, who cast his vote for his friend Taft, Woodrow Wilson won the presidency in 1912. Wilson appointed Franklin K. Lane, a city attorney for San Francisco, as secretary of the interior. Lane quickly approved a bill, the Raker Act, that would permit San Francisco to flood Hetch Hetchy Valley. With a nod from Congress, President Wilson signed the Raker Act into law on December 19, 1913.

An expensive mistake?

His beloved wilderness would soon be gone, and Muir was "sick with exhaustion and grief," writes Ginger Wadsworth in *John Muir: Wilderness Protector*.[23] Almost exactly a year later, in December 1914, Muir was working on a manuscript titled *Travels in Alaska* when he contracted pneumonia. He died in Los Angeles on December 24, 1914, at the age of seventy-six. Though he lost the fight to save Hetch Hetchy Valley, Muir's impassioned writing and political activism awakened the American public to the need to preserve the wilderness. "Saving these woods from the axe and saw, from money-changers and water-changers, and giving them to our country and the world is in many ways the most notable service to God and man," he wrote to his friend William Kent in 1908.[24]

The O'Shaughnessy Dam providing water and hydroelectric power to San Francisco cost over $100 million to build. The first water from Hetch Hetchy arrived in San Francisco in 1934, but by then the city had found a cheaper water source in the Sierra foothills. In retrospect, according to historian Stephen Fox, many people think the Hetch Hetchy dam was an expensive mistake.

The struggle for balance

The long, fierce fight over Hetch Hetchy Valley proved to Muir and other preservationists that saving wild areas would not be easy. Even those who agreed that forests should not be indiscriminately cut and rivers dammed would disagree about how to manage the wilderness. For the next sixty years, the country would struggle to balance nature's preservation with economic and social imperatives.

Other battles would be fought over dams, particularly in the Grand Canyon where the Colorado River has been

Though preservationists lost the battle to prevent construction of the Hetch Hetchy Dam, it was the last dam to be built in a national park.

prized as much for its spectacular beauty as its potential hydroelectric power. In the 1980s, environmentalists would clash with loggers in the national forests over ecosystem protection or timber industry profits.

The Hetch Hetchy controversy highlights the divide between two competing ideals that have shaped American environmental policy: preserving nature for its own sake versus conserving nature as a human resource. As the twentieth century began, the distinction began to blur between the words *preservation* and *conservation*. Yet the divide remained between those who wanted to preserve the wilderness and those who wanted to profit from it.

A footnote to the story of Hetch Hetchy is that the controversy provided new energy for the campaign to save the wilderness. "The preservationists had lost the fight for the valley, but they had gained much ground in the larger war for the existence of wilderness," writes Nash in *Wilderness and the American Mind*.[25] The national parks movement gathered momentum, too, culminating in the creation of the National Park Service in 1916. No dam would ever again be built in a national park.

2

The Creation of the National Parks

FROM ITS BIRTH in 1916, the National Park Service has struggled to satisfy two missions: preserving America's special places for future generations while promoting public use and enjoyment. The National Parks System was created so that unique wilderness areas, natural wonders, and historic sites would not be despoiled. At the same time, the parks were intended for people's use—and people need roads, recreational facilities, campgrounds, and other amenities, which sometimes threaten the ecosystems and wildlife that the Park Service has sought to protect.

The beginning of the park idea

The nineteenth-century artist George Catlin, a well-known painter of the American Indians, is considered one of the earliest proponents of the concept of a national park. On a trip to the Dakotas in 1832, he saw that the pioneer movement was threatening the American Indian civilizations and the wilderness with the onslaught of European culture and values and the killing of wildlife. In Fort Pierre, South Dakota, Catlin saw Sioux Indians killing buffalo to trade with the white men for whiskey, and he feared that both the Indians and buffalo would soon be extinct: "Many are the rudenesses and wilds in Nature's work which are destined to fall before the deadly axe and desolating hands of cultivating man," he wrote.[26] He proposed that the government preserve wilderness areas in parks:

Early proponents of wildlife preservation thought that national parks were the best way to protect the buffalo and Native American civilizations.

What a beautiful and thrilling specimen for America to preserve and hold up to the view of her refined citizens and the world, in future ages! A nation's park, containing man and beast, in all the wild and freshness of their nature's beauty.[27]

Henry David Thoreau also suggested setting "a certain sample of wild nature, a certain primitiveness" for the enjoyment of everyone. "Why should not we . . . have our national preserves . . . in which the bear and the panther, and some even of the hunter race, may still exist, and not be 'civilized off the face of the earth'—our forests . . . not for idle sport or food, but for inspiration and our own true recreation?" wrote Thoreau in the *Atlantic Monthly* in 1858.[28]

In 1864, Vermont congressman George Perkins Marsh published *Man and Nature: Or, Physical Geography as Modified by Human Action*, the first book to analyze humanity's destructive impact on the environment. He criticized clear-cutting forests, the standard logging practice that removes all trees from an area and leaves a checkerboard of woods and stumps, as the cause of drought, flood, erosion, and other ecological disasters. Wilderness preservation was good for the nation's economic well-being, he wrote. Marsh urged the country to keep a large part of "American soil . . . as far as possible, in its primitive condition."[29]

Yosemite Valley sets a precedent

The leading nineteenth-century American landscape architect, Frederick Law Olmsted Jr., designer of New York City's Central Park, joined the campaign to preserve natural areas in the public trust. He advised the government to prevent the nation's most beautiful natural scenes from becoming private property. At the urging of Olmsted and others, Congress in 1864 established the Yosemite Grant, which ceded Yosemite Valley and the nearby Mariposa Big

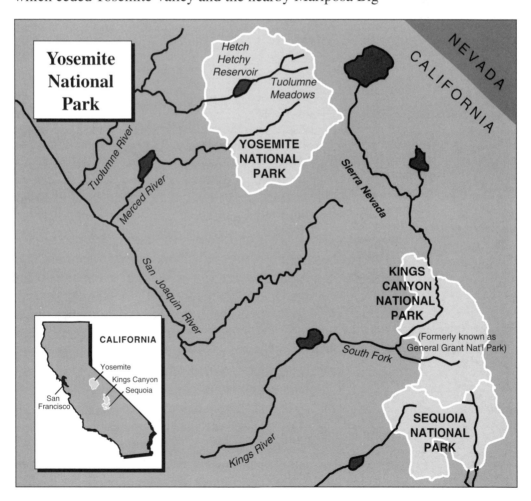

Tree Grove to California as the nation's first state park. These areas would be protected by the state of California and open for public use and recreation. This marked the first time the federal government removed wilderness from development and private ownership.

After a group of well-educated easterners traveled through the Yellowstone wilderness in the Wyoming and Montana Territories in 1870 and discovered the spectacular geysers, hot springs, waterfalls, and colorful Grand Canyon of the Yellowstone River, some of the men suggested the region be exploited for commercial profit. But one man, Yale-educated attorney Cornelius Hedges, advised instead that Yellowstone be set aside as a national park. Since the area was in Wyoming Territory, and not part of a state, the park would be a national park in the custody of the U.S. Department of the Interior.

To safeguard the geysers, scenery, and other natural wonders in the area, Congress made Yellowstone the first national park.

The first national park

But first Congress had to consider the issue. Senators had to be certain that Yellowstone, located in the central Rocky Mountains, was too high and cold for farming or economic development. While the geologic wonders of Yellowstone were obvious, the lawmakers had to be sure that no significant mineral wealth would be lost if the region became a park.

Convinced there was no better use of the land, Congress passed the act establishing Yellowstone country in the territories of Montana and Wyoming "as a public park or pleasuring-ground for the benefit and enjoyment of the people. . . . [The secretary of the interior] shall provide for the preservation . . . of all timber, mineral deposits, natural curiosities, or wonders within said park . . . in their natural condition."[30] President Ulysses S. Grant signed the act on March 1, 1872, creating the first national park in the world.

However, the legislation had a major flaw. No money was allocated to manage Yellowstone and enforce regulations to protect its natural resources. Trappers and hunters continued to kill elk and bison; souvenir hunters stole rock specimens. One spring, some four thousand elk were slaughtered by hide hunters near Mammoth Hot Springs, and cattle continued to use the park for grazing, write Grant W. Sharpe and his coauthors in *A Comprehensive Introduction to Park Management.* Says Sharpe, "The first superintendent of Yellowstone, Nathaniel Langford, was expected to work without a salary. Without funds there was no staff, and without a staff, no law enforcement."[31] Instead, more effort was concentrated on developing hotels, restaurants, and roads.

At 2.2 million acres, or 3,472 square miles, Yellowstone today is one of the few large, natural areas in the lower forty-eight states. With 99 percent of the park undeveloped, the park remains a magnificent wilderness and wildlife refuge, home to brown bear, elk, antelope, moose, lynx, and otter, and 290 species of birds. Yellowstone is also a tourist mecca, with 370 miles of paved roads, 1,200 miles of trails, 9 visitor centers and museums, 9 hotels, 12 campgrounds, and over 2,000 buildings. Even the massive forest fires of 1988, which burned nearly half of Yellowstone, have not kept visitors away.

The parks movement takes off

Yellowstone set the stage for the establishment of other national parks. Four more parks were created in the 1890s: Sequoia and General Grant (the forerunner of Kings Canyon) in California, Mount Rainier in Washington State, and Yosemite. John Muir often led the way.

In the late 1880s, Muir became concerned about logging in Yosemite and overgrazing by flocks of sheep in the high mountain meadows. He feared California was not caring for the park. The glacier-filled lakes, the granite walls of

El Capitan and Half Dome, Yosemite and Bridalveil Falls, and the mountain streams and meadows were too important to be neglected. With support from wilderness advocate Robert Underwood Johnson, editor of *Century* magazine, Muir published articles and lobbied Congress for federal protection of Yosemite Valley. On October 1, 1890, Yosemite National Park was created; sixteen years later, the state preserve was incorporated into the national park, as well.

The parks movement was well on its way. The Antiquities Act of 1906 authorized the president to proclaim features of historic and scientific interest on public lands as national monuments. Beginning with Theodore Roosevelt, presidents used this law to set aside and protect significant natural and historic sites. In 1906, Muir discovered a petrified forest in the Arizona desert. He was shocked to see tourists taking away the petrified logs as souvenirs and mills using the logs as raw materials. "Not one to keep silent, John brought this to public attention," writes Ginger Wadsworth in *John Muir: Wilderness Protector*.[32] Under pressure from Muir, Roosevelt created the Petrified Forest National Monument in December 1906. Also that year, Roosevelt set aside part of the Grand Canyon as a national monument; the Grand Canyon became a national park in 1919 under President Woodrow Wilson. The National Park Service now oversees seventy-three national monuments, including the Statue of Liberty and the Black Canyon of the Gunnison National Monument, a sheer-walled canyon carved by the Gunnison River in Colorado.

Under Roosevelt's administration, five new national parks were created. "There is nothing so American as our parks. The scenery and wildlife are native. The fundamental idea behind the parks is native. It is, in brief, that the country belongs to the people. Parks stand as the outward symbol of this great human principle," said Roosevelt.[33]

The National Park Service

The growing number of national parks were under the authority of the secretary of the interior, but the parks had no central administration to set policy or protect against development. Each park was on its own. At times, the U.S. Army was called in to control poaching and other problems. Yellowstone was managed jointly by the Army Corps of Engineers, the Interior Department, and the park superintendent, an army officer appointed by the secretary of war. No official spokesperson was designated as an advocate for the park system in Washington, D.C. This left the parks vulnerable to competing interests within the Interior Department.

In the early 1900s, a group of private citizens and government officials led by J. Horace McFarland, president of the American Civic Association, began lobbying the White House to form a federal agency to oversee the parks. As the Hetch Hetchy Valley controversy erupted, the parks lobby gained momentum among people concerned that the parks were not being well managed.

The National Park Service was created in 1916 to help manage and protect the growing number of national parks.

In 1915, Stephen Mather, assistant secretary of the interior in charge of parks, and Horace M. Albright, a twenty-five-year-old graduate of the University of California at Berkeley, launched a national publicity campaign urging Americans to vacation in parks and recommending the creation of a park agency. Mather, a wealthy Chicago businessman and outdoorsman, took a group of influential people and journalists, including a congressman, the editor of *National Geographic*, the president of the American Museum of Natural History, and the vice president of the Southern Pacific Railroad, on a tour through Sequoia and Yosemite. He gradually built a coalition to push for a National Parks System.

Congress was convinced the public wanted a national parks agency. On

August 25, 1916, President Woodrow Wilson signed the act establishing the National Park Service, a new federal bureau in the Department of the Interior responsible for managing thirty-five existing national parks and monuments as well as those yet to be established. The act was written by a committee of public officials and private citizens, including Frederick Law Olmsted.

The park system's mission

Under the Park Service's Organic Act, the new agency was directed to

> promote and regulate the use of the Federal areas known as national parks, monuments and reservations . . . by such means and measures as conform to the fundamental purpose of the said parks, monuments and reservations, which purpose is to conserve the scenery and the natural and historic objects and the wild life therein and to provide for the enjoyment of the same in such manner and by such means as will leave them unimpaired for the enjoyment of future generations.[34]

The parks were intended not as pristine wildernesses but as guardians of natural wonders like El Capitan in Yosemite and Old Faithful geyser in Yellowstone. Early supporters of the Park Service, such as Stephen Mather, urged development in the parks for tourism, fishing, and hunting. Yellowstone was considered a hunter's paradise, and the nation's last herds of wild bison were hunted to

The National Park Service oversees some of the vast areas of wilderness managed by the federal government.

near extinction. Soon, roads and tourist amenities were under construction. Wealthy western railroad owners, influential parks supporters, built grand rustic hotels, like El Tovar in the Grand Canyon and the Ahwanee in Yosemite, to entice more Americans to travel by train to the parks.

Five decades later, through the historic Wilderness Act of 1964, Congress was permitted to designate wilderness on federal lands. To win this legislation, the Wilderness Society, a grassroots organization founded in 1935, lobbied Congress for more than eight years, overcoming opposition from mining, timber, and other interests that rely on natural resources.

Under the law, the federal land agencies, including the National Park Service, Forest Service, Fish and Wildlife Service, and Bureau of Land Management, are directed to recommend land under their jurisdiction for designation as wilderness. The properties must be removed from civilization and contain "no commercial enterprise and no permanent road," and be at least five thousand acres in size and of ecological, geological, or scenic value.[35]

Further expansion of preservation efforts

By the late 1990s, the National Wilderness Preservation System encompassed 475 wilderness areas on 104 million acres, including designated wilderness in forty-four units of the park system. Yosemite's total 761,236 acres contain 677,600 acres of wilderness. By law, federal wilderness must be managed to retain its "primeval character and influence, without permanent improvements or human habitation."[36] Mining operations and livestock grazing are allowed if they existed prior to wilderness designation, but commercial enterprise and roads are banned. Some wildernesses, like Yosemite's back country, are open to fishing, hunting, hiking, horseback riding, and primitive camping.

To further expand wilderness protection, Congress established the Wild and Scenic Rivers System in 1968 to help protect free-flowing river systems like the Flathead River on the western boundary of Glacier National Park and Kings River in Kings Canyon National Park, California.

The increasing number of people who vacation in America's parks is making preservation of sensitive areas more difficult.

The rivers, which are in the National Park or National Wildlife Refuge systems, are designated wild, scenic, or recreational, depending on how much development and accessibility is already present. Many of the rivers are critical habitats for trout, salmon, and other fish.

For the people's enjoyment

Before the establishment of Yosemite and Yellowstone National Parks, no large tracts of land had ever been preserved for public enjoyment and wilderness protection. The early advocates of the national parks movement knew they had created what a British ambassador to the United States once called the nation's "best idea." A worldwide national parks movement followed the founding of Yellowstone, and today more than one hundred nations contain more than twelve hundred national parks and preserves.

For the most part, the national parks have been managed for human recreation and pleasure, not for nature and resource protection. Those people who have hiked in the Grand Teton National Park in Wyoming or pitched a tent in Acadia National Park in Maine, driven the foggy ridge of the Great Smoky Mountains National Park in Tennessee or canoed through the swamps and mangrove forests of the Everglades have discovered the parks to be a national treasure and a connection with nature. Not only do they provide enjoyable family vacations, writes Ted Williams in *Audubon*, but the parks offer "the chance to know and understand the things that live and belong in wild places and, even more important, the natural processes by which they function together."[37]

Yet the park system in recent years has increasingly confronted the difficulties of serving as a growing population's national playground, while still safeguarding the vulnerable ecosystems and wildlife that make the national parks so extraordinary.

3

Environmental Activism and Backlash

GROWING ALARM ABOUT vanishing wildlife and wilderness, and the health threats posed to humans from pollutants in the air, water, and earth, led to an overwhelming sense of environmental crisis in the 1960s and 1970s. The bald eagle was on the edge of extinction and the coastal fisheries were dying from overfishing and pollution. Even closer to home for many people was the toxic waste and sludge poisoning the Hudson River in New York and the yellow smog choking Los Angeles. Rachel Carson's 1962 book, *Silent Spring*, about the harmful effects of the widely used pesticide DDT, mobilized public opinion and sparked a new era of environmental activism.

The early conservationists and preservationists were concerned with protecting wildlife, natural resources, and wilderness. Now people were worried about the effects of pollution on human health. While conservationists had historically been in a minority, by the 1970s, more and more people were alarmed about the quality of drinking water and the safety of nuclear power plants. They realized that, by neglecting the natural resources that they relied upon to live, their children's future would be jeopardized. "Millions of people declared themselves environmentalists. The movement exploded," writes Stephen Fox in *The American Conservation Movement*, marked by broad public endorsement

Once on the brink of extinction, the bald eagle has made a comeback due in part to the efforts of environmental activists.

of environmental education and demonstrations such as the annual Earth Day, first commemorated in 1970.[38]

Environmental activism grows

During the 1960s and 1970s, the major environmental groups grew rapidly and wielded growing political influence. No longer on the outside, environmentalists gradually joined the mainstream, finding allies in elected officials who recognized that the environment was a popular issue. Membership in the National Audubon Society, a nonprofit membership group dedicated to saving wildlife habitat, increased from 45,000 in 1965 to 321,500 in 1975. Other groups, like the Wilderness Society and the National Wildlife Federation, also expanded and established visible presences on Capitol Hill.

The Sierra Club, headquartered in San Francisco, grew from 7,000 to 77,000 members during the 1950s and 1960s under the leadership of David Brower, its first executive director. Many people compared Brower, an avid mountaineer who was among the first to scale many western peaks and a tenacious defender of the wilderness, with Sierra Club founder John Muir. Brower spearheaded efforts to create Kings Canyon, North Cascades, and Olympic national parks. Working with the Save-the-Redwoods League and other groups, Brower and the Sierra Club helped slow the destruction of California's redwood trees by pushing for the creation of Redwood National Park in 1968.

To convince more people to support wilderness preservation, Brower launched the Sierra Club book publishing program with a collection of photographs, *This Is the American Earth*, by photographer Ansel Adams, a Sierra Club member since 1919. Two more books by Adams, *The Eloquent Light* and *These We Inherit: The Parklands of*

America, were published in 1962. Adams's stunning black-and-white photographs of Yosemite, Kings Canyon National Park, and other wildlands introduced the American wilderness to millions of people.

In an echo of the Hetch Hetchy dam controversy, in 1964 Brower and the Sierra Club began a successful campaign to protect the Grand Canyon from the U.S. Bureau of Reclamation's plan to build Marble Canyon Dam and a power plant to pump water from the Colorado River to Phoenix. In 1969 the Sierra Club won a lawsuit to stop pollution in Lake Superior. Brower went on to help found three more influential environmental groups, Friends of the Earth, the Earth Island Institute, and the League of Conservation Voters.

Environmentalists and the law

Environmentalists soon discovered the potential of lawsuits to block dams, stop highway projects, close nuclear power plants, and force regulators to tighten pollution controls. By the 1990s, an average of one thousand environmental cases were filed each year in district courts.

In the 1970s, with mounting pressure from environmental groups, and little opposition, Congress overwhelmingly passed major environmental laws. The Clean Air Act in 1970 and the Clean Water Act in 1972 strictly regulated the amount of pollutants released into the environment; in the decades since, air and water quality have significantly improved.

The Sierra Club, the Save-the-Redwoods League, and other conservation groups have helped slow the destruction of California's redwood forests.

Three months before Earth Day 1970, President Richard Nixon signed one of the most important environmental laws, the National Environmental Policy Act of 1969, or NEPA. Federal agencies now had to determine whether a proposal for land use would harm the environment. Along with similar state laws, NEPA gave the public the right to be involved in federal land planning. The law also created regulatory procedures for air and water polluters and required annual reports to the nation on the state of the environment.

Environmentalists have used NEPA to challenge timber harvests and forest management. The Sierra Club used the law to successfully prevent the U.S. Forest Service from allowing a ski resort to be developed in Mineral King Valley, now a part of Sequoia National Park in California.

NEPA also created the Environmental Protection Agency (EPA), the largest government agency, with the mission to "protect human health and to safeguard the natural environment." The EPA supervises state enforcement of federal environmental laws, imposes penalties for violations, researches and funds projects to reduce environmental risk, and provides the public with information on managing human health and environmental risk. President Clinton's proposed EPA budget for 1999 was $7.8 billion, the highest ever.

Junior high school students march during Earth Day 1970.

Vanishing wildlife

As people became more concerned about air and water pollution, they recognized the effects of environmental degradation on wildlife like the bald eagle, once plentiful but nearly extinct by the 1960s. The Endangered Species Act (ESA) of 1973 gave the government the authority to protect, conserve, and propagate species considered to be at risk. By mandating penalties for harming a listed species and requiring a scientific plan to help the species recover, the ESA became a tool for preserving wildlife and stopping development, logging, and grazing on land containing rare plants and animals.

The law has rescued many animals from the brink of extinction, including the red wolf, brown pelican, peregrine falcon, California sea otter, and gray whale. Secretary of the Interior Bruce Babbitt announced in 1998 that the bald eagle population had recovered enough to possibly remove the bird from the ESA list sometime in the next two years.

Humpback whales were nearly hunted to extinction before laws such as the Endangered Species Act went into effect.

Controversy over saving species

But the ESA has been controversial, and opposition has grown with recognition that even little-known species like snail darters are protected. Ranchers, home builders, loggers, and others who make their living from the land say the law blocks economic progress, tramples on property rights, and threatens jobs for minor environmental gains.

In the Southwest, legal battles have raged over plans to halt timber harvests in eleven national forests to protect the Mexican spotted owl and other species. Ranchers along the Gila River in Arizona may have to move their cattle that graze on federal lands with imperiled species like the Apache trout and the loach minnow. "We've fenced streams, spread the cattle out and tried to work with the Endangered Species Act, but they keep coming after us," one unhappy rancher told the *Washington Post* in 1998.[39]

Many environmentalists feel the law does too little and lacks the funding to fulfill its mandate. The ESA targets individual animals, while many people today believe it is more effective to protect larger ecosystems and watersheds. Meanwhile, the list of threatened and endangered plant and animal species grew from 109 names in 1973 to 1,138 (469 animals and 669 plants) in 1998. Almost one in three plant species in the United States is threatened by extinction, according to a 1998 survey. In addition, nearly 4,000 plant and animal species are awaiting review for ESA protection. "With more and more life-forms teetering on the edge, managers struggle with the terrible choice of which ones to throw the lifeline to," writes Douglas H. Chadwick in *National Geographic*.[40]

Since authorizing legislation for the ESA expired in 1993, none of the many attempts to pass a new bill have succeeded in Congress. Even as supporters try to save the law from attacks by its opponents, it remains the last hope for many species and their wild habitats. Mark Van Putten, president of the National Wildlife Federation, described the Endangered Species Act as "the nation's embattled yet enduring shield against wildlife extinction."[41]

The radical environmentalist movement

As the environmental movement widened, some activists in the 1970s and 1980s grew impatient at what they saw as the slow pace of progress in saving natural places. Unwilling to wait for government to tighten regulations, or for lawyers to litigate environmental disputes, these activists— critics call them "ecoterrorists"—decided to take the environment into their own hands, often defying the law.

Earth First!

Direct-action environmentalism soon took off. On a hiking trip in the Mexican desert in late 1979, Dave Foreman, a former lobbyist for the Wilderness Society, his friend Howie Wolke, who worked for Friends of the Earth, wilderness advocate Mike Roselle, and two other environmentalists decided the mainstream environmental movement was too cautious and needed to be shaken up.

The friends formed Earth First!, which they described as a movement, not an organization. Their motto was "No compromise in defense of Mother Earth," even if it meant resorting to "ecotage," the environmental form of sabotage. "The people who started Earth First! decided there was a need for a radical wing that would make the Sierra Club look moderate. Someone has to say what needs to be said, and do what needs to be done and take the kinds of strong actions . . . to dramatize it," recalled Foreman later.[42] He soon became the most visible proponent of Earth First!

Earth First! and similar groups based their ideas about nature on deep ecology, an environmental philosophy first described in 1973 by Norwegian philosopher Arne Naess. Deep ecology goes beyond fighting radiation, toxic waste, and other environmental health hazards. Deep ecologists believe in "biocentrism" instead of "anthropocentrism." That is, human needs, such as jobs or housing, are not as important as restoring the natural world to its wild state. "Earth First! stood for the more radical proposition that the natural world should be preserved for its own sake, not for the sake of any real or imagined benefits to humanity," writes Christopher Manes in *Green Rage*.[43]

Radical environmentalist groups such as Earth First! have targeted ranches where sheep and cattle are allowed to graze on public land.

These radical activists looked to early conservationist Aldo Leopold, the federal forester who campaigned for wilderness preservation in the national forests in the 1920s. In his 1949 book, *A Sand County Almanac*, Leopold, a founder of the Wilderness Society, described what he termed the land ethic, which has become a popular view among environmentalists. "The land ethic simply enlarges the boundaries of the community to include soils, waters, plants, and animals, or collectively: the land," he wrote. Leopold urged Americans to develop an "ecological conscience," or a conviction that each individual is responsible for conserving the land.[44]

Dave Foreman and his friends were also inspired by the southwestern writer and radical conservationist Edward Abbey, who in his 1975 novel *The Monkey Wrench Gang* described a band of environmental guerrillas who sabotaged an industrial development in the Southwest. Abbey once said, "I think we're morally justified to resort to whatever means are necessary in order to defend our land from de-

SPOTTED OWL   COMPROMISE SPOTTED OWL

struction, from invasion."[45] *Monkey-wrenching* became the term Earth First! followers used for environmental sabotage.

Unafraid to put their bodies at risk, Earth First! and other radical environmentalists would lie down on logging roads in Oregon to prevent logging trucks from getting through and cut fences on Wyoming ranches to force grazing cattle off public land.

Redwood Summer

Earth First! made headlines in 1990 when the group organized Redwood Summer to protest logging in the redwood forests in California. Over the past two hundred years, these temperate rain forests with unique ecosystems have shrunk from 2 million acres to about eighty-five thousand, due to harvesting the giant trees for fences and decks. According to *Newsweek*, about 150 old-growth redwoods, valued at $10,000 each, were being felled each day in 1990.

Earth First! targeted a mill owned by Louisiana Pacific, the largest private redwood landholder in the state. Protesters blocked the road to the mill to stop the chain saws. "There's no time left to try to work through legal measures," demonstrator Chris Robinson told *Newsweek*. "You also have to get out and do some grass-roots activism."[46] Forty-four demonstrators were arrested one week for trying to prevent loggers from felling trees.

Other direct-action groups also formed in the 1980s, often created by disillusioned members of mainstream organizations, as Mark Dowie writes in *Losing Ground: American Environmentalism at the Close of the Twentieth Century*. The Sea Shepherd Society, which uses unconventional methods, including damaging ships, to stop seal hunts, illegal whaling, and wolf hunts in British Columbia, was founded by former Greenpeace skipper Paul Watson. The Native Forest Council, an antilogging and forest preservation group, was started by a Sierra Club member in Oregon. A former Wilderness Society employee founded Restore: The North Woods, which works to preserve forests in the Northeast.

Radical environmentalists have been hotly criticized. "These people aren't motivated to save more wilderness. They're more a Marxist organization," declared an Oregon timber industry spokeswoman.[47] Wyoming ranchers, their livestock threatened by the cutting of barbed-wire fences by radical environmentalists in 1998, warned of retaliation. "For their own safety, they better lay off. If the right group finds them, they might get shot," declared one Wyoming rancher.[48]

Even those who support the causes of Earth First! have sometimes questioned its methods. "Redwood Summer was counterproductive. It didn't slow down logging, but it did tend to polarize the community and hand the timber companies a golden opportunity to turn Earth First! into bogeymen," said a Sierra Club leader.[49] Others criticize the dangers posed by monkey-wrenching techniques like tree spikes, which can break the chains of power saws and explode saw blades used in lumber mills. In fact, a large industrial band saw in a northern California mill broke and lacerated a mill worker, possibly because of a spike in the log, Dowie writes. Many Earth First! followers do not condone this type of action.

In the 1990s, Dave Foreman broke with Earth First! and ceased his advocacy of ecoterrorism. In 1995, he was elected to a three-year term as a director of the Sierra Club. Foreman also heads the Wildlands Project, dedicated to restoring and preserving "true wilderness" by establishing wilderness corridors, buffer zones, and other protected habitat for wildlife. "Conservation isn't just about protecting beautiful places or protecting outdoor recreation opportunities. It comes down to protecting the integrity of the diversity of life and the evolutionary process," he told *Sierra* magazine in 1998. His goal remains to "protect as much wilderness and as many intact ecosystems and native species as possible. And as times change as a person changes, you seek new ways of doing that."[50]

Wise use: the antienvironmentalist backlash

In the 1980s, an opposition movement to environmental laws that appeared to restrict commerce, industry, and individual property rights began growing. The root of this opposition movement was the "sagebrush rebellion" of the 1970s when ranchers began protesting federal ownership and control of land in the West. For nominal fees, western ranchers and mining companies had long enjoyed the use of 48 million acres of land administered by the Forest Service, Bureau of Land Management, and other federal agencies. Now, they feared that environmentalists' efforts to preserve open space and save endangered species would deny them their land rights.

This grassroots crusade called itself the wise use movement, a term borrowed from Gifford Pinchot, who described conservation as the "wise use of resources." Followers included western ranchers and cattle associations who feared grazing and irrigation restrictions, loggers who were denied access to national forests, mining interests, and even suburbanites whose backyards were designated critical habitat for endangered species. *The Wise Use*

Agenda: The Citizen's Policy Guide to Environmental Resource Issues, edited by Alan Gottlieb, outlines the goals of the movement:

> The Wise Use Agenda, spread to the widest possible readership and heeded by our national leaders, will go a long way toward correcting the problems of both the environment and overzealous environmentalism. Wise Use will be the environmentalism of the 21st century.[51]

Protests against government land policies have led to violence at times, with several small bombings at Forest Service and Bureau of Land Management facilities, reports Brad Knickerbocker of the *Christian Science Monitor*, who has followed the wise use movement. Wise-users have found support in conservative think tanks, which share their free-market philosophy, and industries that have paid a price for the environmental movement. The automobile industry was compelled to increase pollution controls to comply with the Clean Air Act; developers sometimes had to scrap plans to build in protected wetlands; and manufac-

Followers of the wise use movement believe that resources located on public lands should be made available to loggers, ranchers, and other interests.

turers had to find alternative, often more expensive, ways to dispose of toxic waste than dumping it in rivers.

During the Reagan and Bush administrations of the 1980s and early 1990s, which often opposed environmental regulations, wise use followers became increasingly influential in land-use policy. The Republican-controlled Congress of the mid-1990s launched its own so-called war on the environment, and with the backing of wise use advocates it tried to weaken many environmental laws and regulations, like the Endangered Species Act and Clean Water Act, and slash funding to national parks and the EPA.

The possibility of compromise

If Muir and Pinchot witnessed the first split over wilderness and natural resources policy during the Hetch Hetchy debate, the radical environmentalists and wise use followers squared off over an even deeper chasm. While they both value the natural resources, those who believe wilderness is best left alone have little sympathy with those who claim the right to graze cattle on grasslands, log trees on public lands, or dam rivers to harness hydroelectric power.

Yet some people argue that unless these warring factions work together, they will all lose. Exemplifying the attempt to compromise is one fifth-generation cattle rancher in Douglas, Arizona, who is trying to build bridges between the conflicting interests on western lands. William Mc-Donald, who has 350 head of cattle on 21,000 acres, formed the Malpai Borderlands Group in 1992 to find common ground among ranchers, environmentalists, and government officials. "We are trying to work through the tough issues that tend to divide us in the West—grazing fees, endangered species, growth," said McDonald, who won a MacArthur Fellowship in 1998 for his efforts.[52] Mc-Donald and his fellow ranchers want to maintain their way of life while protecting the land from development and satisfying the concerns of environmentalists. The ranchers have voluntarily agreed to move cattle to maintain vegetation and avoid overgrazing, and to protect ranching areas with endangered species.

4

Doing Business in
the Wilderness

BECAUSE OF THE foresight of early conservationists
and public officials like President Theodore Roosevelt who
valued forests, rivers, and wildlife, hundreds of millions of
acres in the United States have been set aside in national
wildlife refuges, parks, forests, and grasslands, never to be
bulldozed for housing or paved for parking lots.

Within these federal lands, 104 million acres are in the
National Wilderness Preservation System, protected
against logging, road building, and other activities that
would disrupt the pristine wild. But federal wilderness
lands, two-thirds of which lie in remote regions of Alaska,
amount to less than 5 percent of the United States. In fact,
most of the public lands are managed not just as reservations for nature but for recreation, fishing, lumbering, grazing of livestock, and other uses.

Mining, grazing, military activities, hiking, and dirt biking are just some of the uses permitted on lands managed
by the Bureau of Land Management, which oversees 270
million acres under the 1976 Federal Land Policy and
Management Act, requiring the land to be available for
many different uses. Nearly 400,000 miles of road were
cut through national forests to transport logging equip-
ment, while refreshment stands and visitor centers make
the national parks appealing to tourists.

The multiple uses of these lands, while legal, have been
the focus of bitter arguments over environmental issues.

While ranchers and timber companies defend their historic rights to graze cattle on federal grasslands and harvest logs from national forests, environmentalists criticize the federal lands programs for neglecting another function: preserving natural resources for future generations. "Our National Forests are a patchwork of clear cuts; the rivers and streams that run through the forests are polluted and muddied; and critical habitat for endangered wildlife is rapidly disappearing," declared Carl Pope, executive director of the Sierra Club.[53] In 1997, Sierra Club members voted to support legislation to end logging in the national forests.

Activities such as mining, dirt biking, and hiking are permitted on lands administered by the Bureau of Land Management.

Ecosystem preservation vs. timber profits

With their valuable timber and diverse, productive habitats for endangered plants and wildlife, the national forests have been a battleground between conservationists and the timber industry for over a century. The 192-million-acre National Forest System includes 155 forests, from the White Mountain Forest in New Hampshire to the Olympic National Forest in Washington State, and 20 national grasslands. The timber industry uses the forests, which contain 17 percent of the nation's timberlands, as a resource for the paper and building industries. But environmentalists have lobbied for decades to slow down the logging to protect animal habitats, trees, and watersheds.

A look back

Commercial logging in this country began in Maine in the 1800s and moved westward, leaving behind scarred fields filled with ruts and stumps. By the end of the nineteenth century, some people were growing concerned about the erosion, streams polluted with silt, and wasted landscapes left behind by loggers. Fears about watershed protection and forest depletion led Congress to create the first federal forest reserve in Wyoming in 1891.

But federal forest protection would soon mean managing the land for the timber companies. In 1897, President Grover Cleveland signed the Forest Management Organic Act, which preserved and protected 40 million acres of public land as national forests and began the federal timber sales system allowing managed logging in the forests, as well as grazing and mining. The act stated that one of the primary purposes of the forests was "to furnish a continuous supply of timber for the use and necessities of the citizens of the United States."[54]

In 1905, President Roosevelt created the Forest Service, an agency of the U.S. Department of Agriculture, to oversee 86 million wooded acres. The Forest Service had two aims: to conserve forests and supply timber for the nation and to protect watersheds. Gifford Pinchot, the first director of the Forest Service, emphasized his policy of "sustained yield," or scientifically managing forests to ensure timber production and forest health for the long term.

Commercial loggers did not turn to the federal forests until after World War II, when private forests had been substantially logged. Clear-cutting and road building surged, especially in the Pacific Northwest, and the timber industry began to exert more influence on the management of the national forests. "By 1961 clear-cuts had been applied to more than half the harvests in national forests across the country," writes John G. Mitchell in *National Geographic*.[55] By the 1970s, timber sales in the national forests were at an all-time high at 12 billion board feet each year, according to the Forest Service. Today, timber harvest is permitted in 49 million acres of the National Forest System, and about .5 percent of those trees are harvested every year.

Through the federal timber sale program, the industry was able to cut lumber cheaply and sell it for a profit. Yet taxpayers paid the price. During a three-year period in the early 1990s the Forest Service spent $1.3 billion to administer the timber sale program but returned only $300 million to the federal treasury, according to a report by the General Accounting Office. By the late 1970s, the era of unchecked logging was coming to an end. One of the original purposes of the national forests, which contain 2 million acres of ponds and lakes and 200,000 miles of streams and rivers, was watershed protection. National forestlands provide fresh municipal water to about 900 cities and communities. Overcutting harms drinking-water supplies by triggering landslides that pour silt into rivers, as has occurred in Salem, Oregon, in recent years. Valuable fish species such as Pacific salmon and bull trout lose their habitats when rivers fill with silt. Even in the late 1990s,

Unrestrained logging harms drinking-water supplies by clearing trees that would otherwise protect rivers and lakes from landslides.

20 percent of the watersheds near forestlands were in unsatisfactory condition, according to the Forest Service.

Logging slows

Opposition to Forest Service policies grew, and in 1976 Congress passed the National Forest Management Act. "The days have ended when the forest may be viewed only as trees and trees viewed only as timber," said the late Minnesota senator Hubert Humphrey, who wrote the law.[56] The law requires that every national forest have a management plan to regulate wildlife protection, water quality, logging, and other uses. The sale of timber must match the amount that the forest can replace, and the diversity of plant and animal communities has to be protected.

Because of this and other environmental regulations, as well as market conditions, by the 1990s, federal timber sale levels dropped by two-thirds to the pre-1950 levels, and clear-cut harvests were reduced by 80 percent, according to the Forest Service.

The spotted owl

Few fights over the wilderness and federal forests have been as hostile as the one between the timber industry and environmentalists in the old-growth forests of the Pacific Northwest. Only about 5 percent of these ancient forests, which have never been harvested and harbor complex natural communities of plants and animals, remain uncut, and most are in national forests. These woods are considered vital in helping to regulate climate, maintain water levels, prevent flooding, and enrich the soil. The mature trees also offer high-quality lumber to the timber industry.

The battle to save these forests came to focus on the plight of one animal, the northern spotted owl, a nocturnal bird of prey that lives primarily in the ancient forests. The spotted owl builds its nest in dead trees and eats small animals like flying squirrels and mice, which rely on the seeds and nuts of the ancient trees and the decaying forest matter. Because the owl is at the top of the forest food chain, scientists consider it an "indicator species," or early warning

sign that the whole forest is at risk. By the 1970s and 1980s, the owl population was in serious decline.

Under pressure from the Audubon Society, the Sierra Club, and others, the U.S. Fish and Wildlife Service listed the owl as a threatened species under the Endangered Species Act in 1990. This meant that the government had to protect its habitat, the old-growth forests. About 75 percent of the spotted owl habitat is in federal forests.

Earth First! and other radical environmentalists launched a campaign of tree spiking, road blockades, and demonstrations to put the spotted owl in the national spotlight. If the federal government continued to allow logging in old-growth forests, the spotted owl would lose its habitat and die off, they claimed. In 1991, a federal judge halted new timber sales in spotted owl habitat in seventeen national forests until the Forest Service came up with a plan to protect the spotted owl. Loggers and paper-mill workers were outraged that their jobs would be sacrificed to save an animal. Bumper stickers reading "Save a Logger—Eat an Owl" appeared on loggers' pickup trucks in towns like Scotia, California, home of the Pacific Lumber Company's redwood lumber mill.

In 1993, after convening an old-growth-forest conference in Portland, Oregon, with environmentalists and the timber industry, President Clinton announced the 1994 Northwest Forest Plan to slow logging in the last old-growth forests and save the spotted owl. The plan contained economic assistance to logging communities.

But some environmentalists criticized the plan for not doing enough to protect large areas of ancient forests. A study in 1997, funded in part by the Forest Service, found that the spotted owl's population continues to fall.

The timber industry was also far from satisfied. A combination of timber sale reductions, environmental regulations, and a weak market led to the loss of more than thirty thousand timber jobs between 1988 and 1995 in the Northwest. Idaho Forest Industry, Inc., which runs sawmills in Couer d'Alene, Idaho, used to get almost a third of its timber from national forests, but now it gets only 5 percent because of cutbacks by the Forest Service. In the community of Oakridge, Oregon, which depended on logging in old-growth forests, one thousand truckers, mill workers, and loggers were laid off, and stores and businesses lost money. Families even lost their homes and left town looking for jobs elsewhere.

The Tongass

In other parts of the country, the Forest Service has also struggled to achieve its multiple-use mission, as illustrated by the story of one national forest. The 16.9-million-acre Tongass National Forest on the southeastern islands and coast of Alaska is the nation's largest national forest. John Muir called it "a place of endless rhythm and beauty." [57] With its stands of Sitka spruce and Western hemlock, some more than eight hundred years old, this wildland contains one of the world's last temperate-zone rain forests and is home to grizzly bears, bald eagles, salmon, humpback whales, and porpoises.

Yet this federal land also has another function. Nearly a million acres of old-growth forests have been logged in the Tongass since 1954. Starting in the 1950s, the Forest Service spent an average of $55 million a year to subsidize clear-cutting in the Tongass by two large corporations with fifty-year contracts to log over 90 percent of the forest. "They pay as little as $15 for enough wood to build a house. Many trees are ground into pulp and shipped to Japan to make cellophane and disposable diapers," writes Seth Zuckerman in *Saving Our Ancient Forests*. "The clear-cutting of the Tongass destroys rich salmon streams and priceless habitat for grizzly bears and the Sitka black-tailed deer." [58]

Responding to growing public outrage over logging the Tongass, Congress in 1990 set aside 1 million acres as protected wilderness, imposed land management rules in parts of the forests, and reduced federal subsidies to the timber companies. In 1995, the Tongass provided two thousand timber jobs, but the recent closure of two major pulp mills and two sawmills, and the termination of one timber sale contract, has reduced employment. Still, Alaska's congressional delegation wants the Forest Service to guarantee that logging continues and a minimum number of timber jobs remain in the Tongass. The future of the Tongass relies on the Forest Service's long-term management plan, developed in 1997, which sets aside additional areas for wildlife habitat not open to logging and recommends that Congress protect more of the forest's wild rivers. Planning for the Tongass must balance the ecological needs of the forest and economic needs of the local population.

Other natural resources

Lumber is not the only resource that has led to disputes over wilderness lands. The potential for oil recovery in the remote Arctic National Wildlife Refuge, established in 1960, has spawned three decades of conflict between oil developers and environmentalists. The 19.6-million-acre wilderness in northeast Alaska includes barrier islands and coastal lagoons, coastal plain tundra, lakes, mountains, spruce forests, and streams feeding into the Bering Sea.

The refuge, particularly the coastal plain, is rich in wildlife, including tens of thousands of porcupine caribou, which give birth here in June, and millions of migrating snow geese, tundra swans, and other bird species that return to the plain annually from as far away as the Antarctic.

In 1987, the Reagan administration proposed to open the Arctic Refuge to oil and gas drilling. But after the 1989 *Exxon Valdez* tanker spill of 11 million gallons of crude oil into Alaska's Prince William Sound, environmentalists launched a campaign to permanently protect the area as wilderness. A proposal in 1991 to open the refuge to drilling was defeated. But the oil industry has continued to press Congress to pass legislation to open most of the coastal plain to oil drilling. This would mean the construction of roads and pipelines, airstrips and production facilities, and living quarters for thousands of workers.

In 1995 Congress passed a budget bill that included a provision for Arctic oil drilling, but President Clinton objected to the drilling plan and vetoed it. Environmentalists in 1998 are supporting legislation to add the 1.5-million-acre coastal plain to the National Wilderness Preservation System, thus

A worker helps clean up after the 1989 Exxon Valdez *oil spill.*

preventing any further development. "Much of the sense of wilderness would be lost if an oil rig was around the corner," said Roger Kaye, wilderness specialist and pilot in the Arctic National Wildlife Refuge. "The Arctic Refuge is a symbol of the nation's ecological crisis and a symbol of our nation's willingness to leave some places alone." [59]

Forest management for the future

Forest Service chief Michael Dombeck, who took charge in January 1997, says that he wants to manage the forests to protect watersheds and preserve ecosystems while maintaining a stable wood supply and jobs: "We can use the laws that guide our management to advance a new agenda—an agenda with a most basic and essential focus: caring for the land and serving people," he said. [60]

Some people predict that one day the Forest Service will give up its timber sales and look primarily to recreational activities like fishing, hunting, and hiking for revenue. Recreation in the forests can generate thirty-seven times more revenue to the economy than logging, according to Forest Service estimates. Meanwhile, new efforts are under way to save forest wilderness. In 1997, Congresswoman Cynthia McKinney, a Georgia Democrat, introduced the National Forest Protection and Restoration Act to stop logging in national forests. "For decades, the U.S. Forest Service has allowed the timber industry to dominate these forests, while American families are left with stumps, mud slides and polluted drinking water," she said. [61] Then in January 1998, the Clinton administration announced a temporary moratorium on the construction of logging roads in the back country of most national forests until new procedures are in place to protect the environment. The interim rule, opposed by prologging lawmakers and the timber industry, could permanently stop logging on some of the nation's most remote wilderness.

5

Recreation in the Wilderness

THE LONG-TERM IMPACT of the presence of people may be the most damaging to federal wilderness. An estimated 860 million people hike, camp, and drive through the national forests annually, creating a severe stress on the forest ecosystems. The Forest Service predicts the numbers of visitors to the forests will rise to more than a billion each year within the next decade. Likewise, with 265 million visitors in 1997, nearly doubled since the mid-1960s, the national parks have become overwhelmed by their popularity. "Today many national parks, although still beautiful, are marred by teeming, noisy crowds in campgrounds, visitor centers, grocery stores, and restaurants, and by traffic jams on roads and even on trails," writes Richard West Sellars in *Preserving Nature in the National Parks*.[62]

The "ultimate challenge" facing the national parks today is the impact of "too many people and too many cars on the unique natural places," writes Jon Margolis in *Audubon* magazine.[63] Tiny forty-thousand-acre Acadia National Park on the coast of Maine is visited by over 4 million people each year, while 8.7 million flock to the Great Smoky Mountains National Park in Tennessee.

The National Park System was established for "public use and enjoyment," and from its beginnings, those who wanted to preserve the parks' scenic beauty for the pleasure of tourists clashed with others who wanted to protect the ecology of the land. In recent years, the Park Service

OLD FAITHFUL
GEYSER

has increasingly confronted the difficulties of serving as a growing population's national playground while safeguarding the ecosystems and wildlife that make the parks so spectacular.

"Old Faithful" erupts at Yellowstone, one of the nation's most popular national parks.

Even in the early years, park advocates worried about overcrowding and commercialization. In the early 1900s, Yosemite was criticized for its concession stands and bear-feeding stations. When park visits increased sharply following World War II, the situation grew worse. By the 1960s, Yosemite was affected by smog from wood fires and by air pollution caused by traffic jams. Even in the back country, campers and hikers brought urban culture and refuse.

Decades of tight budgets, which have forced the parks to neglect building repairs and capital improvement projects and to manage the parks with lean staffs, have also hampered the Park Service's ability to cope with the crowds. Nevertheless, in the late 1990s, nearly a third of the fifty-four national parks, including Yosemite, launched new efforts to reduce congestion and protect the natural landscapes.

Most people are within a day's drive of a national park, and while automobiles have made the parks accessible to millions, they have created serious problems. By 1997, over 4 million people—almost double the number in 1980—visited Yosemite each year in 1.4 million cars and sixteen thousand tour buses. During peak periods more than six thousand cars inched through bumper-to-bumper traffic as tourists tried to glimpse Half Dome and Bridalveil Falls through car windows and exhaust fumes.

In 1980, the Park Service stated that automobile congestion was the single greatest threat to the Yosemite experience, and it announced a new general management plan to reduce traffic and parking problems.

The plan was slow to be enacted, but in 1997 the Park Service drafted the Yosemite Valley Implementation Plan to help the park reach its 1980 goals. The plan calls for a phased removal of cars, requiring reservations for parking inside the valley boundaries and eliminating day-use auto touring. Eventually, the Park Service expects visitors will leave their cars in nearby towns and use buses to get in and around the park. Visitors will be encouraged to walk, ride a bike, and otherwise experience the valley without the distraction of traffic and

Two skiers enjoy a view of Half Dome unobstructed by traffic and exhaust fumes.

parking. A group of public officials and environmentalists is developing a regional transportation system. The Park Service also expects to remove nonessential buildings, restore parking lots to natural conditions, and reduce the density of campgrounds to ensure the long-term survival of one of the nation's most valued natural treasures.

Traffic control plans are underway in other popular parks. A light rail system will be built outside Grand Canyon National Park, and alternative fuel buses will carry visitors from the rail terminal to locations within the park. Alternative fuel shuttles will also begin operating in Zion National Park in Utah in 2000. "This is welcome news in a place where there are three to four times as many cars as there are parking spaces during the summer season," said Mark Peterson, Rocky Mountains regional director for the National Parks and Conservation Association.[64]

Aviation noise

Audubon writer Margolis notes that the impact of people on the national parks can be felt in many ways, from the eighty thousand snowmobiles that roar through Yellowstone each winter to the personal watercraft that churn up the water and disturb the quiet on Lake Crescent in Washington's Olympic National Park. Environmentalists are seeking a total ban on personal watercraft, known as jet skis, in the park system, but the National Park Service in 1998 said it would continue to allow jet skis in twenty-five sites, while considering over the next two years whether to restrict or ban them in some areas.

Few sights are as awe-inspiring as Arizona's Grand Canyon National Park from the sky above. Many people are

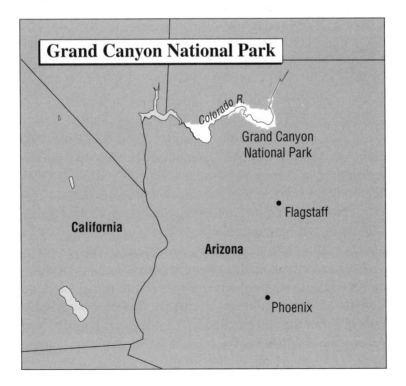

Grand Canyon National Park

Colorado R.

Grand Canyon National Park

Flagstaff

California

Arizona

Phoenix

able to experience this aerial view, thanks to dozens of air tour companies that operate sight-seeing airplanes and helicopters. But the noise from the planes and helicopters has significantly impaired the natural peace of the Grand Canyon and many other parks with tour aircraft. In 1987, Congress passed the National Parks Overflights Act, which banned flights below the canyon's rim and required flight-free zones, in part because of a 1986 midair collision over the Grand Canyon. Some park advocates would like to see even more restrictions on park overflights. "Natural quiet must be protected with the same serious purpose with which we set forth to protect any other natural resource within our national parks," states Senator John McCain (R-Ariz.), author of the 1987 law, in *National Parks* magazine.[65] McCain recently proposed legislation to further restrict overflights.

Islands of wilderness?

The pressures on the national parks come not only from inside their borders. Many parks, forests, and wildlife preserves are surrounded by buffers of wilderness or rural land, which help protect the plants and wildlife. But activities outside the parks threaten the federally protected water, wildlife, and natural landmarks. Grizzly bears in Glacier National Park have lost crucial habitat with construction in nearby wilderness areas. Drainage from sugar plantations has harmed the Everglades National Park in Florida.

Park advocates, like the National Parks and Conservation Association (NPCA), have fought fiercely to limit development and pollution sources near the parks. In 1998, the NPCA convinced a Kentucky judge that a permit for a coal mine adjacent to Cumberland Gap National Historical Park should be rescinded.

Plans to build a large landfill at a remote desert site in California, surrounded on three sides by Joshua Tree National Park, were stopped by a San Diego Superior Court panel in February 1998. The Park Service had lobbied against the two-thousand-acre dump, fearing that the twenty thousand tons of municipal waste that would arrive at the dump each day from all over Southern California

Grand Canyon as seen from the south rim.

would harm the desert's ecosystem and people's wilderness experience, and further endanger the threatened desert tortoise in the region. "We've said all along that it is completely inappropriate to build the country's largest landfill literally in the shadow of one of our most pristine national parks," Brian Huse, a regional director of the NPCA, told a *Washington Post* reporter.[66]

Wildlife on federal land

As the controversy over the spotted owl revealed, one of the most thorny issues in federal land management is wildlife. Wildlife is as important to the survival of ecosystems as are water and trees. Few parks have grappled with this issue as intensely as Yellowstone, where, by the 1920s, park predator control programs using traps, poison, and hired hunters had virtually exterminated mountain lions, wolves, coyotes, cougars, lynx, bobcats, and many other indigenous species. Even pelicans in Yellowstone were viewed as competing with sport fishermen for trout. Recent wildlife management conflicts in the park include the killing by local hunters of Yellowstone bison, which stray outside the park borders, a situation that has provoked outrage from animal rights groups and some environmentalists.

By the 1960s, Yellowstone managers realized that predators such as wolves, which help control the park's elk and bison populations, were critical to the biodiversity and preservation of the park's natural ecosystem. "Without wolves, elk had destroyed the habitat of beaver. When beaver disappeared, wolves could not return," writes Alston Chase in *Playing God in Yellowstone*.[67] The Park Service began a new policy in Yellowstone and other parks to conserve wildlands and animals through natural regulation. Yellowstone staff stopped culling the elk herd and banned the killing of cutthroat trout, an important food source for bears, otters, eagles, and ospreys.

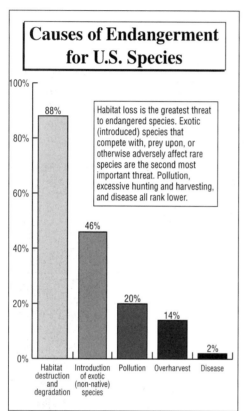

Causes of Endangerment for U.S. Species

Habitat loss is the greatest threat to endangered species. Exotic (introduced) species that compete with, prey upon, or otherwise adversely affect rare species are the second most important threat. Pollution, excessive hunting and harvesting, and disease all rank lower.

Habitat destruction and degradation — 88%
Introduction of exotic (non-native) species — 46%
Pollution — 20%
Overharvest — 14%
Disease — 2%

Source: Environmental Defense Fund.

The gray wolf

But sometimes nature needs help. In 1978, the gray wolf was listed as an endangered species under the Endangered Species Act in all lower forty-eight states except Minnesota. To comply with the ESA's mandate to bring back the gray wolf, the Department of the Interior began a program of wolf reintroduction, releasing thirty-one Canadian wolves into Yellowstone and thirty-five more into central Idaho's Frank Church and River of No Return Wilderness in 1995 and 1996. The program has been successful. The wolves' arrival has benefited Yellowstone's diverse animal population. The wolves, now numbering ninety-seven, have killed many coyotes, allowing other predators to prosper from an increase in rodents usually eaten by coyotes. Meanwhile, the elk population has been checked and the grizzly bears feed on wolf-killed elk.

But neighboring ranchers fear for the safety of their livestock and strongly oppose the program. Several livestock groups, including the American Farm Bureau, went to court to stop it. The National Audubon Society also filed suit, protesting that the wolf reintroduction program did not protect wolves already recolonizing in Idaho. In 1997, a federal judge ruled that the program violated the ESA and ordered the wolves be removed; implementation of the order has been stayed pending an appeal. In fact, the gray wolf is rebounding and may soon be off the protected list.

The future of the parks

The gray wolf in Yellowstone is one of many unresolved issues in the management of the nation's last remaining wildlands, where people, wildlife, and natural resources must somehow coexist. The Park Service today is struggling to maintain its vast properties, which include 376 parks, monuments, battlefields, forts, seashores, and bridges encompassing more than 83 million acres, ranging from the 7-million-acre Gates of the Arctic National Park in Alaska to the Lincoln Memorial in Washington, D.C. As evidence of how far-reaching the system has become, Congress was considering legislation in 1998 to create the newest national park: the National Underground Railroad Network to Freedom, linking four hundred public and private sites, routes, structures, and geographic areas relating to the secret effort to bring thousands of slaves North to freedom in the nineteenth century.

Gray wolves like this one were released into Yellowstone and other parks in order to prevent their extinction.

Yet the parks, coping with a $6 billion backlog in repairs and maintenance and with more visitors each year, cannot be taken for granted. "To most Americans, the opportunity for individual renewal in these protected settings seems an inherent right," writes James Conaway, an expert on western public lands policy, in the *New York Times*. "They are mistaken. The stresses of our age have become manifest in the parks, whose integrity and survival are threatened by intrusive commercialism, legislative manipulation, and institutional poverty."[68] The parks cannot survive without improved management, adequate funding, and public support for initiatives from traffic control policies to increased fees.

6

The Future of Wilderness Management

IN 1997, THE SIERRA CLUB proposed to Congress that the 710-foot-high Glen Canyon Dam, which backed up the Colorado River, flooded Glen Canyon, and created Lake Powell when it was completed in 1963, be demolished. One congressman called the proposal a "bizarre idea," but it is not as far-fetched as it might seem.[69]

In the twentieth century, more than six hundred dams were built with federal funds, mostly in the 1930s, bringing water to the deserts for agricultural development and fueling the growth of Las Vegas, Phoenix, and other desert cities. But the dams destroyed rivers and wildlife habitat, sometimes at a cost outweighing their economic benefits.

A number of dams, whose original purposes had become obsolete, have been demolished in recent years, as people recognize that wild free-flowing rivers prevent natural flooding, keep ecosystems healthy, and allow salmon and other fish to migrate to the sea. "We already spend millions of dollars each year to maintain the Grand Canyon's river ecosystem. Millions are also being spent to protect and restore endangered fish and correct other problems caused by the dam. Why not consider spending the money on restoring the canyon?" asked Daniel P. Beard, a senior vice president of the National Audubon Society.[70] Beard is a former commissioner of the Bureau of Reclama-

An aerial view of the Colorado River and the Glen Canyon Dam (lower left).

tion, which built and operates Glen Canyon Dam. Now he, like David Brower and other environmentalists, is in favor of demolishing it.

Tearing down dams is just one way to restore the wilderness and reestablish species and ecological functions. The need for ecosystem protection has become increasingly urgent. Not only are the ancient forests nearly gone, but in the United States, more than 90 percent of the tallgrass prairies, 55 percent of the wetlands, and 50 percent of tropical forests have been depleted, according to the Nature Conservancy. With increasing pressures on green space, people are trying to protect wildlands and a diversity of plant and animal life, while still allowing economic development and growth.

Sustainable forestry

In the next fifteen years, the demand for paper in the United States is expected to almost double, according to *State of the World 1998: A Worldwatch Institute Report on Progress Toward a Sustainable Society*. Although almost half the paper used in the United States is now recovered through recycling, this growing need for paper will put further claims on the forests.

Although timber companies and environmentalists are often at odds, both agree it is worthwhile to explore logging practices that maintain healthy forests. The timber industry is trying to comply with new environmental regulations and save forest resources for the future.

One approach to achieving healthy, productive, and diverse forest ecosystems is sustainable forest management. Sustainable forestry practices aim to maintain the complete forest ecosystem to meet the social, economic, and ecological needs for the present and future. Instead of clear-cutting all trees in an area, which damages watersheds and habitats, loggers identify individual mature trees to remove. Trees that die before maturity are not harvested but left on the forest floor as habitat for insects and fungi. Low-impact harvesting techniques, like horse logging, are also preferred over trucks and logging roads.

Sustainable forestry success and the Collins-Almanor Forest

The American Forest and Paper Association, which represents the paper and solid wood industry, made a formal commitment to sustainable forestry in 1994 and pledged to practice a "land stewardship ethic" that integrates the management and harvesting of trees for useful products with "the conservation of soil, air, and water quality, wildlife and fish habitat, and aesthetics."[71] The Forest Service is experimenting with sustainable forestry in some of its lands.

The Collins-Almanor Forest, a ninety-four-thousand-acre commercial forest owned by the Collins Pine Company in northeastern California, has operated under a sustained yield management plan since the 1940s. The forest contains mixed stands of ponderosa pine, sugar pine, Douglas fir, white fir, and incense cedar. Trees are selected individually to harvest. The harvest is planned to sustain the balance between vegetation and wildlife, which includes the black bear, raccoon, coyote, beaver, mountain lion, rainbow trout, red-tailed hawk, and California spotted owl. To meet the requirements of laws protecting endangered species, the company does not cut trees containing visible nests, and random thickets of trees are left uncut for habitat cover and stream protection.

Certified forests

The Collins-Almanor Forest, which won a 1996 Presidential Award for Sustainable Development from President Bill Clinton, is one of a growing number of forests certified as sustainable. In 1993, the Forest Stewardship Council (FSC), an international nonprofit organization, developed certification standards for sustainable forests. The certification allows wood and paper companies to sell products with labels stating that the wood was harvested from a well-managed forest. The idea is that people will not mind paying more for products made with the least harm to forests.

Habitat conservation plans

Other efforts are also being made to improve the management of wildlands. A controversial new approach for protecting animal habitats has proliferated in the 1990s. First authorized by Congress in 1982 as a modification of the Endangered Species Act, habitat conservation plans (HCPs) are zoning and ecosystem-protection agreements between the federal government and private landowners. HCPs provide real estate developers, timber and mining companies, and individual property owners with a special permit to commit an "incidental take" of one or more endangered species in the course of conducting business. In exchange, the landowners must devise a plan that minimizes or mitigates the damage, such as protecting or reclaiming habitat elsewhere. Approximately two hundred plans, covering more than 6 million acres of land, had been authorized by the Interior Department by 1998. Secretary of the Interior Bruce Babbitt has called HCPs "a quiet revolution in American conservation."[72]

This kind of long-term bargain alarms many environmentalists. A group of scientists wrote to Congress in July 1996 protesting that habitat conservation plans were being approved with too little scientific research and oversight, Jon Luoma writes in *Audubon* magazine. The environmental group Defenders of Wildlife issued a report in 1998 challenging HCPs for allowing habitat destruction without adequately protecting plant and animal species that may be endangered in the future. "The next 40 years of scientific research will certainly produce new data and insights. One need only consider the change in science's understanding of spotted owls and other species affected by the proposed HCP in the last 40 years," stated a recent scientific study by the Audubon Society.[73]

Nature Conservancy

While the federal government struggles to balance wilderness protection and economic parity, conservation groups are working to save wildlands and stem suburban sprawl through innovative financing plans and land management agreements.

Donations from private landowners have been critical to save natural places from destruction. In the western corner of Susquehanna County, Pennsylvania, lies the 650-acre Woodbourne Forest Preserve, with its stands of Eastern hemlock, ash, maple, and oak trees, some over four hun-

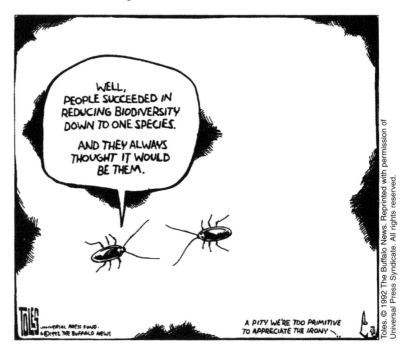

dred years old. In 1956, the Francis Cope family, a local Quaker family, donated the property to the Nature Conservancy, a private nonprofit group that protects plants, animals, and natural communities by preserving the land and water. "Part of what's important is we've got segments of deep dark woods. There are species of animals which require deep forest interiors," says forest naturalist Jerry Skinner. "We keep the trails clean and that's about it. The forest floor is littered. Whenever a tree goes down it stays there because it's habitat."[74]

Founded in 1951, the Nature Conservancy acquires land through exchanges, gifts, conservation easements, management agreements, purchases, and other kinds of partnerships. Staff and volunteers manage many of the preserves, which are generally open to the public for hiking, bird watching, photography, and other low-impact uses. To date, the conservancy has protected over 9 million acres of ecologically significant land, including, most recently, prairie and grasslands in North Dakota, wetlands in Illinois, and red rock country in southeastern Utah.

Natural areas like Walden Pond State Reservation (pictured) are being preserved with help from taxpayers and state aid.

Linking wildlands

Protecting tracts of land is a beginning. The next step is linking the green spaces to reestablish extensive natural habitats. Too often, roads, logging, development, and other encroachments fracture ecosystems into small isolated units, leaving many native species at risk. Since the early 1980s, roadkills have been responsible for nearly two-thirds of all deaths of Florida panthers, an endangered species whose habitat has been largely broken up and lost.

Across the country, conservation groups and state agencies are working together to create wildlands corridors—networks of green space that allow wildlife to migrate, feed, mate, and thrive—and eco-regions, or large natural areas with management and restoration plans. The state of Florida and the Nature Conservancy are collaborating to acquire and protect a wildlands corridor stretching from the Everglades in South Florida to the Okefenokee Swamp on the Georgia border.

In other parts of the country, environmentalists are looking at large-scale ecosystem preservation. When Yellowstone National Park was created in 1872, its boundaries were arbitrarily drawn to include the ten thousand geothermal geysers and basins, disregarding animal habitats and the larger ecosystem. In 1983, the Greater Yellowstone Coalition was formed by one hundred regional and national groups to preserve the Greater Yellowstone Ecosystem, which covers some 18 million acres of public and private lands in Wyoming, Idaho, and Montana. This is one of the world's last large, mostly intact ecosystems in the northern temperate zone. But it is threatened by habitat fragmentation from development, overgrazing, logging, road building, and the impact of 200,000 residents and 3 million annual visitors. The coalition is trying to preserve the region by controlling oil and gas exploration, mining, logging, and development.

Taxpayers say "yes" to open space

In fact, taxpayers, like those in Florida who support the wildlands corridor, are increasingly willing to pay the price to preserve open space. In May 1998, New Jersey governor Christine Todd Whitman unveiled a plan to preserve 1 million acres of open space and farmland in New Jersey over the next decade. Her plan relies on raising $1.6 billion by hiking the state gasoline tax and other new fees, and by contributions from local governments as well as land donations from private owners willing to sell below appraised value. No tax increases are popular. Nevertheless, Whitman's plan was approved by voters in November 1998.

Voters in California, Florida, Texas, Georgia, New York, and other states have also agreed to higher taxes to protect green space and watersheds from development. Across the country in 1996 and 1997, voters approved nearly three out of four of more than 150 environmental financing measures calling for a small property or sales tax. Together, these measures will raise more than $4 billion for conservation projects.

In addition, as people in more states look for ways to save green space, environmental victories are increasingly found locally—a wetland saved from development in one community; a field that could one day return to forest preserved in another; or the dedication of a new neighborhood park.

The newest national parks

Meanwhile, at the national level, efforts to extend the protective reach of the federal land agencies progress slowly. Each year Congress considers new proposals for national parks, wildlife refuges, and designated wilderness areas.

One of the most significant recent expansions of federal land protection came in 1994 with the passage of the California Desert Protection Act. This landmark legislation, which took seven years to win congressional approval, protects 6.37 million acres of California desert, formerly managed by the Bureau of Land Management, through the creation of two new national parks—Death Valley and Joshua Tree—and one national preserve—the Mojave. Within those areas, the act designated 3.5 million acres of land as protected wilderness.

The California deserts contain many mountain ranges, dry lakes, badlands, mesas, buttes, lava beds, sand dune systems, and other fragile ecosystems. But mining, grazing, urban development, recreation, and vandalism have posed increased threats to the land and the hundreds of desert wildlife species like the desert tortoise. With the new federal protections, the deserts will be able to recover and survive. "This area of the country contains some of the most extraordinary resources in the nation. The scenic, recreational, cultural and scientific value of the California desert must be preserved. We cannot afford to lose these resources, which deserve protection as part of the national park and national wilderness system," said Senator Dianne Feinstein (D-Calif.), who sponsored the bill.[75]

The Omnibus Park Act of 1996 created the Tallgrass Prairie National Preserve to help restore eleven thousand acres of the vanishing tallgrass prairie in Kansas and the Opal Creek Wilderness in Oregon. The same year, President Bill Clinton signed a proclamation creating the 1.7-million-acre Grand Staircase-Escalante National Monument on the Colorado Plateau in south-central Utah. The Bureau of Land Management is charged with protecting the area's red rock canyons, rare rock formations and high cliffs, one-thousand-year-old piñon and juniper plants, prehistoric dwellings, examples of ancient rock art, fossils, and hundreds of species of birds, amphibians, mammals, and reptiles.

Thousands more acres of land have been proposed as parks and wilderness areas and await congressional action. Wilderness advocates have identified more than 100 million acres in Idaho, Montana, the Pacific Northwest, the southern Appalachians, Alaska, and other regions that would benefit from federal wilderness designation.

Yet obstacles remain, as Congress weighs competing interests for uses of the land. The Grand Staircase-Escalante National Monument was considered by the Park Service to be unique and in need of federal protection. But the remote region also harbors large underground coal reserves and many Utah residents bitterly opposed the designation, which blocked plans for coal mine development.

The California Desert Protection Act of 1994 designated 3.5 million acres of desert as protected wilderness.

Financing, too, is often an obstacle. The Land and Water Conservation Fund (LWCF) has been a resource since 1964 for purchasing national park, forest, and wildlife refuge lands. The fund is supported through offshore oil and gas royalties that companies contribute in exchange for drilling permits.

Since the 1960s, the LWCF, administered by the Park Service, has helped pay for 7 million acres of parklands and thirty-seven thousand recreation projects, including the Cape Cod National Seashore and the New Jersey Pinelands National Reserve. But Congress usually appropriates less than the $900 million authorized amount. Since the 1980s, over $11 billion from the fund has been funneled into other parts of the federal budget, according to the Sierra Club. Park advocates criticize what they term a lack of foresight to protect wildlands. "Failure to protect our open spaces exacts a high price. In the nation's 222-year history, we have destroyed half our wetlands. Between 1982 and 1992, more than 5.5 million acres of privately-owned forest land has been lost," states Jean Hocker, president of the Land Trust Alliance, in defense of full funding of the LWCF. "Today's investments in conservation will pay enormous dividends far beyond our lifetimes."[76]

Adirondacks: forever wild

In the northeast corner of New York State lies one of the largest wilderness areas in the United States. Mountains, four thousand lakes and ponds, the source of the Hudson River, and vast pristine forests compose the 6-million-acre Adirondack Park. What makes this wilderness unique, and vulnerable, is that about 58 percent of the land is privately owned. The state owns 2.5 million acres of public forest preserve, while 3.5 million acres of the park are in commercial timberland, estates, camps, and 110 villages and towns.

Between 1885 and 1894, New York lawmakers passed a series of laws and constitutional amendments that deemed that the lands of the Adirondack Forest Preserve "shall be forever kept as wild forest lands," never to be "leased, sold, or exchanged, or be taken by any corporation, public

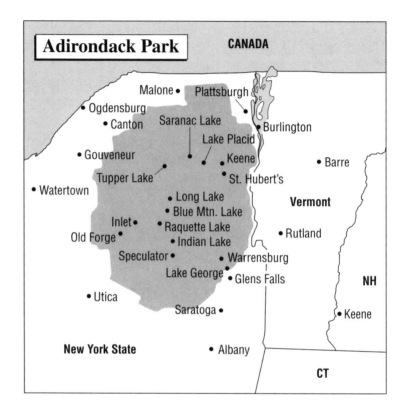

Adirondack Park

CANADA

Malone • Plattsburgh

• Ogdensburg

• Canton Saranac Lake

Lake Placid

• Gouveneur • Keene • Burlington

Tupper Lake • St. Hubert's • Barre

• Watertown • Long Lake Vermont

• Blue Mtn. Lake

Inlet • • Raquette Lake • Rutland

Old Forge • • Indian Lake

Speculator • • Warrensburg

Lake George • • Glens Falls NH

• Utica

Saratoga • • Keene

New York State • Albany

CT

or private.[77] Adirondack Park was officially set aside in 1892. By the late nineteenth century, the region had already been heavily logged and cleared for iron mines and farms. The topsoil was eroded and the region frequently flooded. The tanning and paper industries were polluting the soil and water.

Those who wanted to protect the Adirondacks back then were not primarily concerned about preserving wildlife habitat or saving the trees, as Paul Schneider chronicles in *The Adirondacks: A History of America's First Wilderness*. They were worried about what would happen if the forest was cut; worried they would be left with a dry useless desert; worried the water supply would dry up and flooding caused by log drivers would dislodge sediment in the Hudson River, which would clog up the river and even the New York Harbor downstream.

Then, as now, people realized that despoiling a wilderness would result in more than the loss of trees. Ravaging the Adirondacks' wild heritage would devastate the ecosystem and economics of an entire region. But it has not been easy to manage a public-private park like the Adirondack.

In 1971, the state created the Adirondack Park Agency to develop long-range land-use plans for public and private land in the park. Gradually, over the years, the state added to the original acreage, buying up key parcels of private land and acquiring conservation easements to protect land adjacent to timberland.

Economic struggles in the Adirondacks

Yet the recent history of the Adirondacks has been racked "by accounts of skirmishes between the land-use agency and adversarial developers, politicians and property rights groups," writes John G. Mitchell in *National Geographic*.[78] The region has been struggling economically, putting added pressures on the land preservation efforts. The logging industry, which once dominated the economy, has been on a downturn in the 1990s, and jobs are hard to find. A controversy in 1997 over plans to build a maximum-security prison within the park in Tupper Lake, New York, highlighted the tension between economic realities and park preservation. The prison would bring nearly four hundred jobs to the region, but park advocates worried about its environmental impact.

John Muir once wrote,

> The tendency nowadays to wander in wilderness is delightful to see. Thousands of tired, nerve-shaken, over-civilized people are beginning to find out that going to the mountains is going home; that wildness is a necessity; and that mountain parks and reservations are useful not only as fountains of timber and irrigating rivers, but as fountains of life.[79]

Even as new battles are being fought over development and preservation in the Adirondacks, the message is clear: Whatever happens in the Adirondacks and other surviving American wilderness lands will affect us all.

Notes

Introduction

1. Quoted in John Naar and Alex J. Naar, *This Land Is Your Land: A Guide to North America's Endangered Ecosystems*. New York: HarperPerennial, 1992, p. 65.

2. Marjory Stoneman Douglas, *The Everglades: River of Grass*. New York: Rinehart, 1947, p. 385.

Chapter 1: Preservation vs. Conservation

3. John Muir, "Features of the Proposed Yosemite National Park," *Century* magazine, vol. 40, no. 5, September 1890. Available at www.sierraclub.org/john_muir_exhibit/writings/features_of_the_proposed_yosemite_national_park.

4. Muir, "Features of the Proposed Yosemite National Park."

5. David Dobbs and Richard Ober, *The Northern Forest*. White River Junction, VT: Chelsea Green, 1995, p. xvii.

6. Quoted in Roderick Nash, *Wilderness and the American Mind*. New Haven, CT: Yale University Press, 1967, pp. 23–24.

7. Nash, *Wilderness and the American Mind*, p. 24.

8. Ralph Waldo Emerson, *Selected Writings of Ralph Waldo Emerson*, ed. William H. Gilman. New York: Signet, 1983, p. 193.

9. Quoted in Nash, *Wilderness and the American Mind*, p. 102.

10. Henry David Thoreau, *Walden, or Life in the Woods and On the Duty of Civil Disobedience*. New York: New American Library, 1960, p. 128.

11. Henry David Thoreau, *The Selected Works of Thoreau*. Boston: Houghton Mifflin, 1975, p. 672.

12. John Muir, "The American Forests," *Our National Parks*. San Francisco: Sierra Club Books, 1991, pp. 268–69.

13. Muir, "The American Forests," p. 272.

14. Quoted in H. W. Brands, *T. R.: The Last Romantic*. New York: Basic Books, 1997, p. 24.

15. Quoted in Lois Markham, *Theodore Roosevelt*. New York: Chelsea House, 1985, p. 93.

16. Brands, *T. R.*, p. 622.

17. Quoted in Brands, *T. R.*, p. 624.

18. Quoted in Stephen Fox, *The American Conservation Movement: John Muir and His Legacy*. Madison: University of Wisconsin Press, 1985, p. 144.

19. Quoted in *John Muir, a Sierra Club Historical Profile*. San Francisco: Sierra Club Member Services, 1998.

20. Gifford Pinchot, *Breaking New Ground*. New York: Harcourt Brace, 1947, pp. 243–44.

21. Quoted in Nash, *Wilderness and the American Mind*, p. 161.

22. Quoted in Fox, *The American Conservation Movement*, p. 140.

23. Ginger Wadsworth, *John Muir: Wilderness Protector*. Minneapolis: Lerner, 1992, p. 140.

24. Quoted in James M. Morley, *Muir Woods*. San Francisco: Smith-Morley, 1991, p. 6.

25. Nash, *Wilderness and the American Mind*, p. 180.

Chapter 2: The Creation of the National Parks

26. Quoted in Nash, *Wilderness and the American Mind*, p. 101.

27. Quoted in Naar and Naar, *This Land Is Your Land*, p. 243.

28. Quoted in Nash, *Wilderness and the American Mind*, p. 102.

29. Quoted in Nash, *Wilderness and the American Mind*, p. 105.

30. Quoted in Nash, *Wilderness and the American Mind*, p. 108.

31. Grant W. Sharpe et al., *A Comprehensive Introduction to Park Management*. Champaign, IL: Sagamore, 1994, pp. 10–11.

32. Wadsworth, *John Muir*, p. 118.

33. Quoted in National Parks and Conservation Association, *Our Endangered Parks*. San Francisco: Foghorn Press, 1994, p. 18.

34. Quoted in National Park Service, *The National Parks: Index 1997–1999*. Washington, DC: U.S. Department of the Interior, 1997, p. 6.

35. Quoted in National Park Service, *The National Parks*, p. 8.

36. Quoted in National Park Service, *The National Parks*, p. 8.

37. Ted Williams, "Deregulating the Wild," *Audubon*, July/August 1997, p. 58.

Chapter 3: Environmental Activism and Backlash

38. Fox, *The American Conservation Movement*, pp. 291–92.

39. Tom Kenworthy, "In Desert Southwest, a Vigorous Species Act Endangers a Way of Life," *Washington Post*, February 1, 1998, p. A03.

40. Douglas H. Chadwick, "Dead or Alive: The Endangered Species Act," *National Geographic*, March 1995, p. 15.

41. Mark Van Putten, "More Peril for Endangered Species," *National Wildlife*, February/March 1998, p. 8.

42. Quoted in Christopher Manes, *Green Rage: Radical Environmentalism and the Unmaking of Civilization*. Boston: Little, Brown, 1990, p. 70.

43. Manes, *Green Rage*, p. 71.

44. Aldo Leopold, *A Sand County Almanac*. 1949. Reprint, New York: Ballantine Books, 1984, p. 239.

45. Quoted in Manes, *Green Rage*, p. 175.

46. Quoted in Bill Barol, "Eco-Activist Summer," *Newsweek*, July 2, 1990, p. 60.

47. Quoted in Manes, *Green Rage*, p. 154.

48. Quoted in James Brooke, "In New Wild West, It's Cowboys vs. Radical Environmentalists," *New York Times*, September 20, 1998, p. 31.

49. Quoted in Tom McKusick, "The Changing Face of Earth First!" *Utne Reader*, January/February 1991, p. 31.

50. Quoted in B. J. Bergman, "Wild at Heart," *Sierra*, January/February 1998, pp. 28, 115.

51. Alan Gottlieb, ed., *The Wise Use Agenda: The Citizen's Policy Guide to Environmental Resource Issues*. Bellevue, WA: Free Enterprise Press, 1989.

52. Quoted in Mindy Sink, "Preserving His Home on the Range," *New York Times*, June 14, 1998, p. BU12.

Chapter 4: Doing Business in the Wilderness

53. Carl Pope, "National Forests at the Crossroads" (June 29, 1998). Available at www.sierraclub.org/forests/report.html.

54. Quoted in Nash, *Wilderness and the American Mind*, p. 137.

55. John G. Mitchell, "Our National Forests: In the Line of Fire," *National Geographic*, March 1997, p. 70.

56. Quoted in Mitchell, "Our National Forests," p. 86.

57. Quoted in Naar and Naar, *This Land Is Your Land*, p. 194.

58. Seth Zuckerman and the Wilderness Society, *Saving Our Ancient Forests*. Los Angeles: Living Planet Press, 1991, p. 49.

59. Telephone interview with Roger Kaye, July 23, 1998.

60. Quoted in B. J. Bergman, "Lay of the Land," *Sierra*, July/August 1998, p. 21.

61. Cynthia McKinney, "Introduction of National Forest Protection and Restoration Act to Congress," October 31, 1997. Available at www.ezl.com/ppg/transcri.html.

Chapter 5: Recreation in the Wilderness

62. Richard West Sellars, *Preserving Nature in the National Parks*. New Haven, CT: Yale University Press, 1997, p. 2.

63. Jon Margolis, "With Solitude for All," *Audubon*, July/August 1997, p. 46.

64. Quoted in National Parks and Conservation Association press release, "Park Advocacy Group Calls Transportation Program First Step in Solving National Park Congestion," November 25, 1997.

65. John McCain, "Overflight Oversight," *National Parks*, September/October 1997, p. 42.

66. Quoted in Rick Weiss, "Landfill Blocked for Desert Site Near U.S. Park," *Washington Post*, February 20, 1998, p. A21.

67. Alston Chase, *Playing God in Yellowstone*. Boston: Atlantic Monthly Press, 1986, p. 136.

68. James Conaway, "Still Our Best Idea," *New York Times*, May 25, 1998, p. A15.

Chapter 6: The Future of Wilderness Management

69. Quoted in Andrew Murr and Sharon Begley, "Dams Are Not Forever," *Newsweek*, November 17, 1997, p. 70.

70. Daniel P. Beard, "Dams Aren't Forever," *New York Times*, October 6, 1997, p. A19.

71. The American Forest and Paper Association, "Principles for Sustainable Forestry," December 1995. Available at www.afandpa.org/Forestry/principles.html.

72. Quoted in Jon R. Luoma, "Habitat-Conservation Plans: Compromise or Capitulation?" *Audubon*, January/February 1998, p. 38.

73. Quoted in John H. Cushman Jr., "The Endangered Species Act Gets a Makeover," *New York Times*, June 2, 1998, p. 2.

74. Telephone interview with Jerry Skinner, June 9, 1998.

75. Quoted in "California Desert Protection Act" (June 9, 1998). Available at www.senate.gov/~feinstein/desert.html.

76. Quoted in "Land Trust Alliance" website (June 3, 1998). Available at www.lta.org/news.html.

77. Quoted in John G. Mitchell, "A Special Place: Adirondack High," *National Geographic*, June 1998, p. 120.

78. Mitchell, "A Special Place," p. 131.

79. Muir, *Our National Parks*, p. 1.

Organizations
to Contact

Earth First!
Earth First! Journal
P.O. Box 1415
Eugene, OR 97440
(541) 344-8004

This radical environmental movement conducts direct-action campaigns in defense of the last wild places like the old-growth forests of the Pacific Northwest. Followers of Earth First! use a combination of education, litigation, and civil disobedience, like tree sitting and roadblocking, to stop logging in the ancient forests. Earth First! has no central staff or office. To find out about the movement, people may contact *Earth First! Journal*, published eight times a year, which includes information on Earth First! and other radical environmental groups.

Environmental Defense Fund (EDF)
257 Park Ave. South
New York, NY 10010
(212) 505-2100
Internet: www.edf.com

Founded in 1967 to ban the pesticide DDT, the 300,000-member Environmental Defense Fund has a staff of scientists, lawyers, and economists who conduct research and litigate to find solutions to environmental problems. Some of the issues EDF works on include global warming, acid rain, and rain forest destruction. In recent years, EDF has become a leading advocate of economic incentives to solve environmental problems. EDF recently helped develop a plan to restore 420,000 acres of wetlands, forests, and native grasses along the

Minnesota and Illinois Rivers by paying farmers to retire flood-prone and eroding cropland along the rivers and to re-create natural buffer zones to prevent agricultural runoff.

Friends of the Earth
1025 Vermont Ave. NW, Suite 300
Washington, DC 20005-6303
(202) 783-7400
Internet: www.foe.org

Friends of the Earth, founded by David Brower in 1969, is a national nonprofit advocacy group that promotes biological, cultural, and ethnic diversity, and helps citizens participate in improving the environment. The organization focuses on political and economic issues affecting the environment. Its report, *Green Scissors '98*, targets seventy-one federal programs and subsidies that hurt the environment and cost taxpayers nearly $50 billion.

League of Conservation Voters (LCV)
1707 L St. NW, Suite 550
Washington, DC 20036
(202) 785-8683
Internet: www.lcv.org

The LCV, founded in 1970, is a nonpartisan political organization dedicated to educating citizens about the environmental voting records of members of Congress. Each year, the LCV publishes the *National Environmental Scorecard*, which details how elected officials voted on environmental legislation.

National Audubon Society
700 Broadway
New York, NY 10003
(212) 979-3000
Internet: www.audubon.org

The National Audubon Society works to conserve and restore natural ecosystems, especially the habitats of birds and other wildlife. Founded in 1905 by conservationists concerned about the killing of birds for hat plumes, the group is named for John James Audubon, ornithologist, explorer, and wildlife artist. With 550,000 members in 508 chapters nationwide, the society manages 100 Audubon sanctuaries and nature centers, and campaigns to restore endangered species, preserve endangered forests, protect wildlife refuges, restore water flows, and protect corridors for migratory birds.

National Parks and Conservation Association
101 Thirty-First St. NW
Washington, DC 20007
(202) 944-8530
Internet: www.npca.org

The association is the foremost advocacy group for the national parks. The private, nonprofit membership association founded in 1919 to defend and promote the park system keeps track of park legislation and park planning issues, from jet ski restrictions to visitors' fees, and helps resolve problems in the national parks. *National Parks* magazine is the only national publication focusing solely on the national parks.

National Wildlife Federation (NWF)
1400 Sixteenth St. NW
Washington, DC 20036
(202) 797-6800
Internet: www.nwf.org/nwf/

The National Wildlife Federation is the largest member-supported conservation group. Founded in 1936 by editorial cartoonist J. N. "Ding" Darling, NWF currently reports over 4 million members and forty-six state affiliates. NWF's primary focus is protecting wildlife, wild places, and the environment through education. Issues include water quality, endangered habitats, wetlands, and land stewardship through legal and grassroots advocacy. The organization publishes books and magazines and runs hands-on nature programs for children, students, and families.

Nature Conservancy
1815 North Lynn St.
Arlington, VA 22209

(703) 841-5300

Internet: www.tnc.org

The mission of the Nature Conservancy, founded in 1951, is to preserve plants and animals by protecting their land and water habitats. The conservancy has protected more than 9 million acres in the United States and Canada; the private nonprofit organization owns and manages more than sixteen hundred nature preserves across the country. The conservancy also works with partners in Latin America and around the world to preserve wild places.

Sierra Club

730 Polk St.

San Francisco, CA 94109

(415) 776-2211

Internet: www.sierraclub.org

The Sierra Club is one of the oldest nonprofit, membership-supported organizations promoting conservation of the natural environment. Founded in 1882 by John Muir, the 630,000-member Sierra Club works to save the environment by education, outreach, and political lobbying. The club has sixty-five chapters in the United States and Canada. The group also sponsors hikes and outings in the wilderness for members.

Wilderness Society

900 Seventeenth St. NW

Washington, DC 20006

(202) 833-2300

Internet: www.wilderness.org

The Wilderness Society was founded in 1935 with the aim of preserving the American wilderness. The society was largely responsible for the passage in 1964 of the Wilderness Act, the law that designates and protects wilderness areas on federal lands. The national nonprofit membership organization is devoted to saving wilderness and wildlife; protecting prime forests, parks, rivers, deserts, and shore lands, and fostering an American land ethic.

Suggestions for Further Reading

Books

Nathan Aaseng, *Jobs vs. the Environment: Can We Save Both?* Hillside, NJ: Enslow, 1994.

Virginia Alvin and Robert Silverstein, *The Spotted Owl.* Brookfield, CT: Millbrook Press, 1994.

Tricia Andryszewski, *The Environment and the Economy: Planting the Seeds for Tomorrow's Growth.* Brookfield, CT: Millbrook Press, 1995.

Steven H. Dashefsky, *Environmental Literacy: The A-to-Z Guide.* New York: Random House, 1993.

Marjory Stoneman Douglas, *The Everglades: River of Grass.* Sarasota, FL: Pineapple Press, reprint 1997.

Trent Duffy, *The Vanishing Wetlands.* New York: Franklin Watts, 1993.

Lois Markham, *Theodore Roosevelt.* New York: Chelsea House, 1985.

Douglas T. Miller, *Henry David Thoreau: A Man for All Seasons.* New York: Facts On File, 1991.

John Muir, *Our National Parks.* San Francisco: Sierra Club Books, 1991.

Dorothy Hinshaw Patent, *Habitats: Saving Wild Places.* Hillside, NJ: Enslow, 1993.

Geoffrey C. Saign, *Green Essentials: What You Need to Know About the Environment.* San Francisco: Mercury House, 1994.

Peter K. Schoonmaker, *The Living Forest*. Hillside, NJ: Enslow, 1990.

Jenny Tesar, *Shrinking Forests*. New York: Facts On File, 1991.

Ginger Wadsworth, *John Muir: Wilderness Protector*. Minneapolis: Lerner, 1992.

———, *Rachel Carson: Voice for the Earth*. Minneapolis: Lerner, 1992.

Websites

Environmental News Network
www.enn.com

This site presents daily environmental news and information from many media outlets. Special reports on the ocean, sperm whales, forest certification, and other current issues also appear.

National Park Service
www.nps.gov

The National Park Service's webstite offers information on the park system's mission and history, current legislation, planning and development, and more. Facts about individual parks are also available.

U.S. Environmental Protection Agency (EPA)
www.epa.gov

The EPA's website is a useful resource on environmental laws and regulations. EPA projects are highlighted. The site's EPA Student Center provides current research material on environmental topics from acid rain to which states recycle the most waste.

U.S. Forest Service
www.fs.fed.us

This website is a good source of information and news on the federal forests. Forest Service reports and press releases are available. Information on individual forests can also be accessed.

Works Consulted

American Forest and Paper Association, "Principles for Sustainable Forestry," December 1995. Available at www.afandpa.org/Forestry/principles.html.

Associated Press, "Certified Forests Are Viewed as Way to Help Conservation," *New York Times*, December 26, 1997.

Bill Barol, "Eco-Activist Summer," *Newsweek*, July 2, 1990.

Daniel P. Beard, "Dams Aren't Forever," *New York Times*, October 6, 1997.

B. J. Bergman, "Wild at Heart," *Sierra*, January/February 1998.

———, "Lay of the Land," *Sierra*, July/August 1998.

H. W. Brands, *T. R.: The Last Romantic.* New York: Basic Books, 1997.

James Brooke, "In New Wild West, It's Cowboys vs. Radical Environmentalists," *New York Times*, September 20, 1998.

Lester Russell Brown, *State of the World, 1998: A Worldwatch Institute Report on Progress Toward a Sustainable Society.* New York: W. W. Norton, 1997.

Rachel Carson, *Silent Spring.* New York: Houghton Mifflin, 1962.

Douglas H. Chadwick, "Dead or Alive: The Endangered Species Act," *National Geographic*, March 1995.

———, "Return of the Gray Wolf," *National Geographic*, May 1998.

Alston Chase, *Playing God in Yellowstone.* Boston: Atlantic Monthly Press, 1986.

James Conaway, "Still Our Best Idea," *New York Times*, May 25, 1998.

John H. Cushman Jr., "U.S. to Suspend Road Building in Many National Forest Areas," *New York Times*, January 10, 1998.

———, "Courts Expanding Efforts to Battle Water Pollution," *New York Times*, March 1, 1998.

———, "The Endangered Species Act Gets a Makeover," *New York Times*, June 2, 1998.

———, "E.P.A. and States Found to Be Lax on Pollution Law," *New York Times*, June 7, 1998.

Roger L. DiSilvestro, *Reclaiming the Last Wild Places: A New Agenda for Biodiversity*. New York: John Wiley & Sons, 1993.

David Dobbs and Richard Ober, *The Northern Forest*. White River Junction, VT: Chelsea Green, 1995.

Mark Dowie, *Losing Ground: American Environmentalism at the Close of the Twentieth Century*. Cambridge, MA: MIT Press, 1996.

Ralph Waldo Emerson, *Selected Writings of Ralph Waldo Emerson*. Ed. William H. Gilman. New York: Signet, 1983.

Stephen Fox, *The American Conservation Movement: John Muir and His Legacy*. Madison: University of Wisconsin Press, 1985.

Carey Goldberg, "Downsizing Activism: Greenpeace Is Cutting Back," *New York Times*, September 16, 1997.

Alan Gottlieb, ed., *The Wise Use Agenda: The Citizen's Policy Guide to Environmental Resource Issues*. Bellevue, WA: Free Enterprise Press, 1989.

Frank Graham Jr., "Earth Day 25 Years," *National Geographic*, April 1995.

Jonathan Harr, *A Civil Action*. New York: Vintage Books, 1996.

John Muir, a Sierra Club Historical Profile. San Francisco: Sierra Club Member Services, 1998.

Tom Kenworthy, "In Desert Southwest, a Vigorous Species Act Endangers a Way of Life," *Washington Post*, February 1, 1998.

Aldo Leopold, *A Sand County Almanac*. 1949. Reprint, New York: Ballantine Books, 1984.

Jon R. Luoma, "Habitat-Conservation Plans: Compromise or Capitulation?" *Audubon*, January/February 1998.

Christopher Manes, *Green Rage: Radical Environmentalism and the Unmaking of Civilization*. Boston: Little, Brown, 1990.

Jon Margolis, "With Solitude for All," *Audubon*, July/August 1997.

John McCain, "Overflight Oversight," *National Parks*, September/October 1997.

Cynthia McKinney, "Introduction of National Forest Protection and Restoration Act to Congress," October 31, 1997. Available at www.ezl.com/ppg/transcri.html.

Tom McKusick, "The Changing Face of Earth First!" *Utne Reader*, January/February 1991.

John McPhee, *Encounters with the Archdruid*. New York: Noonday Press and Farrar, Straus and Giroux, 1971.

John G. Mitchell, "Our National Forests: In the Line of Fire," *National Geographic*, March 1997.

————, "A Special Place: Adirondack High," *National Geographic*, June 1998.

James M. Morley, *Muir Woods*. San Francisco: Smith-Morley, 1991.

John Muir, "Features of the Proposed Yosemite National Park," *Century* magazine, vol. 40, no. 5, September 1890. Available at www.sierraclub.org/john_muir_exhibit/writings/features_of_the_proposed_yosemite_national_park.

Andrew Murr and Sharon Begley, "Dams Are Not Forever," *Newsweek*, November 17, 1997.

John Naar and Alex J. Naar, *This Land Is Your Land: A Guide to North America's Endangered Ecosystems*. New York: HarperPerennial, 1992.

Roderick Nash, *Wilderness and the American Mind*. New Haven, CT: Yale University Press, 1967.

National Parks and Conservation Association, *Our Endangered Parks*. San Francisco: Foghorn Press, 1994.

National Parks and Conservation press release, "Park Advocacy Group Calls Transportation Program First Step in Solving National Park Congestion," November 25, 1997.

National Park Service, *The National Parks: Index 1997–1999*. Washington, DC: U.S. Department of the Interior, 1997.

Gifford Pinchot, *Breaking New Ground*. New York: Harcourt Brace, 1947.

Carl Pope, "National Forests at the Crossroads" (June 29, 1998). Available at www.sierraclub.org/forests/report.html.

Jennifer Preston, "Battling Sprawl, States Buy Land for Open Space," *New York Times*, June 9, 1998.

John F. Reiger, *American Sportsmen and the Origins of Conservation*. Norman: University of Oklahoma Press, 1986.

Paul Schneider, *The Adirondacks: A History of America's First Wilderness*. New York: Henry Holt, 1997.

———, "Clear Progress: 25 Years of the Clean Water Act," *Audubon*, September/October 1997.

Richard West Sellars, *Preserving Nature in the National Parks*. New Haven, CT: Yale University Press, 1997.

Grant W. Sharpe et al., *A Comprehensive Introduction to Park Management*. Champaign, IL: Sagamore, 1994.

Mindy Sink, "Preserving His Home on the Range," *New York Times*, June 14, 1998.

Henry David Thoreau, *Walden, or Life in the Woods and On the Duty of Civil Disobedience*. New York: New American Library, 1960.

———, *The Selected Works of Thoreau*. Boston: Houghton Mifflin, 1975.

USDA Forest Service, Tongass Land Management Planning Team, *Tongass Forest Plan Review*, June 1997.

Mark Van Putten, "More Peril for Endangered Species," *National Wildlife*, February/March 1998.

Rick Weiss, "Landfill Blocked for Desert Site Near U.S. Park," *Washington Post*, February 20, 1998.

Ted Williams, "Deregulating the Wild," *Audubon*, July/August 1997.

Seth Zuckerman and the Wilderness Society, *Saving Our Ancient Forests*. Los Angeles: Living Planet Press, 1991.

Index

Picture Credits

About the Author

Ann Malaspina has written on many topics, including law, housing, immigration, culture, and education, for newspapers, magazines, and reference books. She holds a B.A. in English from Kenyon College and an M.S. in journalism from Boston University. Her first book for Lucent Books, *Children's Rights*, was published in 1998. She lives in New Jersey with her husband, Robert Harold, an attorney with the New York Legal Aid Society, and their two sons, Samuel and Nicholas.